LIFE TOGETHER STUDENT EDITION

SERVING

OTHERS IN LOVE

LIFE TOGETHER STUDENT EDITION

SERVING

OTHERS IN LOVE

6 small group sessions
on ministry

Doug Fields &
Brett Eastman

ZONDERVAN.com/
AUTHORTRACKER
follow your favorite authors

We want to hear from you. Please send your comments about this
book to us in care of zreview@zondervan.com. Thank you.

ZONDERVAN

SERVING Others in Love: 6 Small Group Sessions on Ministry
Copyright © 2003 by Doug Fields and Lifetogether™

YS Youth Specialties is a trademark of YOUTHWORKS!, INCORPORATED and is registered with the United
States Patent and Trademark Office.

Requests for information should be addressed to:

Zondervan, *Grand Rapids, Michigan 49530*

Library of Congress Cataloging-in-Publication Data

Fields, Doug, 1962–
    Serving others in love : 6 small group sessions on ministry / by Doug
Fields and Brett Eastman.— 1st ed.
      p. cm.
    Summary: Presents lessons to be used by small groups to explore ways to serve Jesus through prayer,
scripture, fellowship, and ministry.
      ISBN 978-0-310-25336-5 (pbk.)
      1. Christian life—Juvenile literature. 2. Christian teenagers—Religious life—Juvenile literature. [1.
Christian life. 2. Teenagers—Religious life.] I. Eastman, Brett, 1959- II. Title.
    BV4531.3.F543 2003
    259'.23—dc21
                                              2003005873

Concept and portions of this curriculum are from Doing Life Together (Zondervan, 2002), used by permission
from Brett & Dee Eastman, Karen Lee-Thorp and Denise & Todd Wendorff.

Cover and interior design: Tyler Mattson, NomadicMedia.net

Printed in the United States of America

ACKNOWLEDGMENTS

I'm thankful to the adult volunteers at Saddleback Church who are great small group leaders and to the students who are growing spiritually because they're connected to other believers. Good things are happening, and I'm so proud of you!

I'm thankful to the team at www.simplyyouthministry.com for working so hard to help create these types of resources that assist youth ministers and students throughout the world.

Gratitude for help on this project goes to Dennis Beckner, Kathleen Hamer, Erica Hamer, and especially Matt McGill who read every word of each book in the series and has made a big difference in my life and the books I write. What a joy to do life together with friends!

—DF

CONTENTS

Welcome to a relational journey!

My prayer is that this book, a few friends, and a loving adult leader will take you on a journey that will revolutionize your life. The following six sessions were designed to help you grow as a Christian in the context of a caring, spiritual community. This community is a group of people committed to doing life together, at least for a season of your life. Spiritual community is formed when each small group member focuses on Jesus and the others in the group.

Creating spiritual community isn't easy. It requires trust, confidentiality, honesty, care, and commitment to meet regularly with your group. These are rare qualities in today's world. Any two or three people can meet together and call it a group, but it takes something special from you to create a community in which you can be known, be loved, be cared for, and feel safe enough to reveal thoughts, doubts, and struggles and still to be yourself. You may be tempted to show up at the small group session and sit, smile, and be nice, but never speak from your heart or say anything that would challenge another group member's thinking. This type of superficial participation prevents true spiritual community.

Most relationships never get beneath the relational surface. This LIFETOGETHER series is designed to push you to think, to talk, and to open your heart. You'll be challenged to expose some of your fears, hurts, and habits. As you do this, you'll find healing, experience spiritual growth, and build lasting, genuine friendships. Since God uses people to impact people you'll most likely become a richer, deeper, more vibrant person as you experience LIFETOGETHER with others. If you go through this book (and the 5 other books in this series) you will become a deeper and stronger follower of Jesus Christ. Get ready for something big to happen in your life!

WHAT YOU'LL FIND IN EACH SESSION

For each session, the group time contains five sections, one for each of the primary biblical purposes: fellowship, discipleship, ministry, evangelism, and worship. The five purposes can each stand alone, but when they're fused together, they make a greater impact on you and your world than the five of them might if approached separately. Think about it like this: If you play baseball or softball, you might be an outstanding hitter, but you also need to be able to catch, throw, run, and slide. You need more than one skill to make an impact for your team. In the same way, the five purposes individually are good, but when you put them all together, you're a balanced player who makes a huge impact.

The material in this book (and the other LIFETOGETHER books) is built around God's Word. You'll find a lot of blank spaces and journaling pages where you can write down your thoughts about God's work in your life as you explore and live out God's purposes.

Here's a closer look at what you'll find in these five sections:

FELLOWSHIP: CONNECTING Your Heart to Others'
[goal: to have students share about their lives and listen attentively to others]

These questions give you and the members of your small group a chance to share from your own lives, to get to know one another better, and to offer initial thoughts on the session theme. The picture for this section is a heart because you're opening up your heart so others can connect with you on a deeper level.

DISCIPLESHIP: GROWING to Be Like Jesus
[goal: to explore God's Word, learn biblical knowledge, and make personal applications]

This is the time to explore the Bible, gain biblical knowledge, and discuss how God's Word can make a difference in your life. The picture for this section is a brain because you're opening your mind to learn God's Word and ways.

You'll find lots of questions in this section; more than you can discuss during your group time. Your leader will choose the questions your group will discuss. You can respond to the other questions on your own during the week, which is a great way to get more Bible study. (See **At Home This Week** on page 27.)

MINISTRY: SERVING Others in Love
[goal: to recognize and take opportunities to serve others]

During each small group session, you'll have an opportunity to discuss how to meet needs by serving others. As you grow spiritually, you'll begin to recognize—and take—opportunities to serve others. As your heart expands, so will your opportunities to serve. Here, the picture is a foot because you're moving your feet to meet the needs of others.

EVANGELISM: SHARING Your Story and God's Story
[goal: to consider how the truths from this lesson might be applied to our relationships with unbelievers]

It's too easy for a small group to become a clique and only care about one another. That's not God's plan for us. He wants us to reach out to people with the good news. Each session will give you an opportunity to discuss your relationships with unbelievers and consider ways to reach out to them. The picture for this section is a mouth because you're opening your mouth to have spiritual conversations with unbelievers.

WORSHIP: SURRENDERING Your Life to Honor God
[goal: to focus on God's presence]

Each small group session ends with a time of prayer. You'll be challenged to slow down and turn your focus toward God's love, his goodness, and his presence in your life. You'll spend time talking to God, listening in silence, and giving your heart to him. Surrender is giving up what you want so God can give you what he wants. The picture for this section is a body, which represents you surrendering your entire life to God.

AT HOME THIS WEEK

At the end of each session, you'll find reminders of ways you can help yourself grow spiritually until your small group meets again. You're free to vary the options you choose from week to week. You'll find more information about each of these options near the end of the first session.

Daily Bible Readings

Page 112 contains a list of Bible passages to help you continue to take God's Word deeper in your life.

Memory Verses

On page 116 you'll find six Bible verses to memorize, one related to the topic of each session.

Journaling

You're offered several options to trigger your thoughts, including a question or two related to the topic of the session. Journaling is a great way to reflect on what you've been learning or to evaluate it.

Wrap It Up

Each session contains a lot of discussion questions, too many for one small group meeting. So you can think through your answers to the extra questions during the week.

LEARN A LITTLE MORE

You might want to learn a little more (hey, great title for a subsection!) about terms and phrases in the Bible passage. You'll find helpful information here.

FOR FURTHER STUDY

One of the best ways to understand Bible passages is by reading other verses on the same topic. You'll find suggestions here.

BEING IN A SMALL GROUP

You probably have enough casual or superficial friendships and don't need to waste your time cultivating more. To benefit the most from your small group time and to build great relationships, here are some ideas to help you:

Prepare to participate

Interaction is a key to a good small group. Talking too little will make it hard for others to get to know you. Everyone has something to contribute—yes, even you! But participating doesn't mean dominating, so be careful to not monopolize the conversation! Most groups typically have one conversation hog, and if you don't know who it is in your small group, then it might be you. Here's a tip: you don't have to answer every question and comment on every point. The bottom line is to find a balance between the two extremes.

Be consistent

Healthy relationships take time to grow. Quality time is great, but a great *quantity* of time is probably better. Plan to show up every week (or whenever your group plans to meet), even when you don't feel like it. With only six sessions per book, if you miss just two meetings you'll have missed 33 percent of the small group times for this book. When you make a commitment to your small group a high priority, you're sure to build meaningful relationships.

Practice honesty and confidentiality

Strong relationships are only as solid as the trust they are built upon. Although it may be difficult, take a risk and be honest with your answers. God wants you to be known by others! Then respect the risks others are taking and offer them the same love, grace, and forgiveness God does. Make confidentiality a nonnegotiable value for your small group. Nothing kills community like gossip.

Come prepared

You can always arrive prepared by praying ahead of time. Ask God to give you the courage to be honest and the discipline to be respectful of others.

You aren't required to do any preparation in the workbook before you arrive (unless you're the leader—and then it's just a few minutes). But you may want to work through the **Growing** questions before your group time. Talk about this idea with your leader. If your group is going to do this, don't view the preparation as homework but as an opportunity to learn more about yourself and God to prepare yourself to go deeper.

Congratulations...

...on making a commitment to go through this material with your small group! Life change is within reach when people are united through the same commitment. Your participation in a small group can have a lasting and powerful impact on your life. Our prayer is that the questions and activities in this book help you grow closer to the other group members, and more importantly, to grow closer to God.

Doug Fields & Brett Eastman

Doug and Brett were part of the same small group for several years. Brett was the pastor of small groups at Saddleback Church where Doug is the pastor to students. Brett and a team of friends wrote Doing LifeTogether, a group study for adults. Everyone loved it so much that they asked Doug to revise it for students. So even though Brett and Doug both had a hand in this book, it's written as though Doug were sitting with you in your small group. For more on Doug and Brett see page 144.

FOR SMALL GROUP LEADERS

As the leader, prepare yourself by reading through the lesson and thinking about how you might lead it. The questions are a guide for you to help students grow spiritually. Think through which questions are best for your group. No curriculum author knows your students better than you. This small amount of preparation will help you manage the time you'll have together.

How to Go through Each Lesson

This book was written to be more like a guidebook than a workbook. In most workbooks, you're supposed to answer every question and fill in all the blanks. In this book, there are lots of questions and plenty of space.

Rule number one is that there are no rules about how you must go through the material. Every small group is unique and will figure out its own style and system. (The exception is when the lead youth worker establishes a guideline for all the groups to follow. In that case, respect your leader and conform your group to the leader's guidelines).

If you need a standard to get you started until you navigate your own way, this is how we used the material for a 60-minute session.

Intro (4 minutes)
Begin each session with one student reading the **Small Group Covenant** (see page 96). This becomes a constant reminder of why you're doing what you're doing. Then have another student read the opening paragraphs of the session you'll be discussing. Allow different students to take turns reading these two opening pieces.

Connecting (10 minutes)
This section can take 45 minutes if you're not careful to manage the time. You'll need to lead to keep this segment short. Consider giving students a specific amount of time and hold them to it. It's always better to leave students wanting more time for an activity than to leave them tired and bored.

Growing (25 minutes)
Read God's Word and work through the questions you think will be best for your group. This section will usually have more questions than you are able to discuss. Before the small group begins, take time to read through the questions to choose the best ones for your group. You may want to add questions of your own.

Serving and Sharing (10 minutes)
We typically choose one of these two sections to skip if pressed for time. If you decide to skip one or the other, group members can finish the section on their own during the week. Don't feel guilty about passing over a section. One of the strengths of this material is the built-in, intentional repetition. You'll have other opportunities to discuss that biblical purpose.

Surrendering (10 minutes)
We always want to end the lesson with a focus on God and a specific time of prayer. You'll be given several options, but you can always default to your group's comfort level to finish your time.

Closing Challenge (1 minute)
We encourage the students to pick one option from the **At Home This Week** section that they'll do on their own. The more often students are able to take the initiative

and develop the habit of spending time with God, the healthier they will be in their spiritual journey. We've found that students have plenty of unanswered questions that they want to go back and consider on their own.

Keep in Mind

- The main goal of this book isn't to have group members answer every question. The goal is **spiritual growth.**
- Make whatever adjustments you think are necessary.
- It's your small group, it's your time, and the questions will always be there. Use them, ignore them, or assign them to be answered during the week.
- Don't feel the pressure to have everyone answer every question.
- Questions are a great way to get students connecting to one another and God's Word.

Suggestions for Existing Small Groups

If your small group has been meeting for a while and you've already established comfortable relationships, you can jump right into the material. Make sure you take the following actions, even if you're a well-established group:

- Read through the **Small Group Covenant** on page 96 and make additions or adjustments.
- Read the **Prayer Request Guidelines** together (on page 128). You can maximize the group's time by following these guidelines.
- Consider whether you're going to assign the material to be completed (or at least thought through) before each meeting.
- Familiarize yourself with all the **At Home This Week** options that follow each lesson. They are detailed near the end of Session 1 (page 27) and summarized after the other five lessons.

Although handling business like this can seem cumbersome or unnecessary to an existing group, these foundational steps can save you from headaches later because you took the time to create an environment conducive to establishing deep relationships.

Suggestions for New Small Groups

If your group is meeting together for the first time, jumping right into the first lesson may not be your best option. You might want to have a meeting before you begin going through the book so you can get to know each other. To prepare for the first gathering, read and follow the **Suggestions for Existing Groups.**

When you get together with your group members, spend time getting to know one another by using ice-breaker questions. Several are listed here. Pick one or two that will work best for your group. Or you may have ice breakers of your own that you'd like to use. The goal is to break ground in order to plant the seeds of healthy relationships.

Ice Breakers

What's your name, school, grade, and favorite class in school? (Picking your least favorite class is too easy.)

Tell the group a brief (basic) history of your family. What's your family life like? How many brothers and sisters do you have? Which family members are you closest to?

What's one thing about yourself that you really like?

Everyone has little personality quirks—strange and unique habits that other people usually laugh about. What are yours?

Why did you choose to be a part of this small group?

What do you hope to get out of this small group? How do you expect it to help you?

In your opinion, what do you think it will take to make our small group work?

Great resources are available to help you!

Companion DVDs are available for the LifeTogether small group books. These DVDs contain teaching segments you can use to supplement each session by playing them before your small group discussion begins or just prior to the Growing to Be Like Jesus discussion. Some of my favorite youth ministry communicators in the world are included on these DVDs. (See page 140.)

In addition to the teaching segments on the DVDs, we've added small group leader tips that are unique to each session. Brett and I give you specific small group pointers and ideas that will help you lead each session. If you spend five to 10 minutes watching the leadership tips and then spend another 10 to 15 minutes reading through each session in advance, you'll be fully equipped to lead students through the material. The DVDs aren't required, but they're a great supplement to the small group material.

In addition, you can find free, helpful tips for leading small groups on our Web site, www.simplyyouthministry.com/lifeto-gether. These tips are general, so any small group leader may benefit from them.

I encourage you to take advantage of these resources!

What STARTING TO GO WHERE GOD WANTS YOU TO BE is all about

Starting to Go Where God Wants You to Be begins with a call to love God and love others, followed by one session on each of the five biblical purposes: fellowship, discipleship, ministry, evangelism, and worship. It's like a table set with great appetizers. You get to taste them all.

I encourage small groups to begin with Starting to Go Where God Wants You to Be. Then study the rest of the books in any order—maybe by interest, maybe in an order that prepares you for events on the youth ministry calendar, such as Sharing Your Story and God's Story before an evangelism outreach in the fall or Serving Others in Love to prepare for the mission trip in the spring. With five other books to choose from, you're in control. There's no "correct" order for using the books.

You're ready to get started!

LIFE TOGETHER STUDENT EDITION

SERVING

OTHERS IN LOVE

YOU ARE GOD'S MASTERPIECE

As a freshman in high school, I began to follow God's ways and soon after felt God prompting me not to waste my life. When I was first introduced to the idea of serving, I knew I needed to. By the time I was a senior in high school I was working with the junior high ministry at my church. The fact that I was doing *anything* to express my love for God is a testimony of God's transforming work in me!

God used the youth minister at my church to recognize my potential and challenge me to serve as an act of obedience to God. God also used my small group leader to show me that God doesn't have to wait for followers to become perfect before he can use them. This guy's personal life was a mess, yet he served God by mentoring and discipling me throughout my high school years. As I reflect, I can see a lot of reasons why I began serving God at a relatively young age. Through them all God was at work, developing me into a person who ministers to others.

That's his goal for you too.

Since my teenage years, I've seen thousands of students develop their gifts and serve in many ministries. Some have taught children's Sunday school. Others have led junior high small groups. I've seen them stack chairs, greet peers as they arrive at youth group, write dramas, pick up trash, and play in the band. Regardless of their tasks, they had hearts sensitive to serving God.

You can serve in many ways, but one common truth binds all the opportunities together: God designed you to spend your life serving him. It may not be in a full-time, paid job or even within the local church, but you *were* created to serve. Don't waste your life sitting on the sidelines watching God's work. Instead get in the game and be part of God's plan. Your small group get-togethers and this book are two tools that God wants to use to help you discover your gifts and develop your passion to serve others. You're in for an exciting journey!

LOWSHIP: CONNECTING Your Heart to Others'

[goal: to have students share about their lives and listen attentively to others]

Name one thing you love to do that you're pretty good at.

Here are some ideas to get you thinking: singing, acting, making friends, playing sports, writing, caring for children, leading, talking, helping others, creating, dancing, building, setting up for an activity, teaching, and listening.

Can you imagine a way God can use you doing what you're pretty good at within the church? If yes, how? If no, why not?

If you haven't discussed the **Small Group Covenant** on page 96, take time to read it together and discuss it now. Make commitments to one another that your group time will reflect those values. You may want to have one person read the covenant to the group before you begin each lesson as a reminder.

Use the **Small Group Roster** (page 98) to record the names and contact information of the small group members.

DISCIPLESHIP: GROWING to Be Like Jesus

[goal: to explore God's Word, learn biblical knowledge, and make personal applications]

Congratulations! You're an original masterpiece! There is no one just like you! You're a unique individual, and God has great plans for your life. God doesn't *need* anyone to accomplish the work of his kingdom, but his plan is still to use you and me. He has something special he wants to do through you!

13For you created my inmost being;
    you knit me together in my mother's womb.
14I praise you because I am fearfully and wonderfully made;
    your works are wonderful,
    I know that full well.
15My frame was not hidden from you
    when I was made in the secret place.
When I was woven together in the depths of the earth,
16   your eyes saw my unformed body.
All the days ordained for me
    were written in your book
    before one of them came to be.

—Psalm 139:13-16

Terms that look like this are described in **Learn a Little More** near the end of the session.

Since God doesn't make any mistakes or have any accidents, why do so many people have a hard time recognizing their worth?

Most Christians understand that God has created everyone, but why do Christians struggle with devaluing one another?

Since God created you, then why do you have so many faults and hang-ups (as we all do)?

What's one thing you don't like about how God created you?

7

Verse 16 reads, "All the days ordained for me were written in your book before one of them came to be." What's your initial response to this?
- What are the implications for your life?

8

What could your youth group look like if everyone treated one another as wonderful creations of God? What would change this week if everyone took this seriously?

9

10

Read Ephesians 2:8-10.

> **8For it is by grace you have been saved, through faith—and this not from yourselves, it is the gift of God—9not by works, so that no one can boast. 10For we are God's workmanship, created in Christ Jesus to do good works, which God prepared in advance for us to do.**
> —Ephesians 2:8-10

- What does it mean to be God's workmanship?
- Since we've been saved by faith, why does God want us to do good works?

MINISTRY: SERVING Others in Love

[goal: to recognize and take opportunities to serve others]

The goal of this lesson is to get you thinking about serving in a ministry. Consider the opportunities that are currently available and consider creating new options for serving.

You may choose an area to serve in and later realize it's not a good match. For instance, you may decide to teach third grade Sunday school and a month later say, "I have the gift of teaching, but those animals don't have the gift of listening." That's okay. Take that as a cue to either learn more skills to make you a better teacher and come back to it later or experiment with a different ministry opportunity.

On the other hand, don't give up on a ministry too quickly. Give yourself time to adjust before you decide whether it's a good fit. If you jump from one ministry to another too often, you'll get discouraged and may develop a reputation for being uncommitted.

List three ministry opportunities you would like to get involved with or start.

Take a few minutes and go through the following checklist of questions with each of the ideas you listed above.

Depending on the size of your small group and the time you have remaining, you may want to do this on your own or in groups of two or three.

◇ What would you need from God to help you succeed with this idea?

◇ What is it about this ministry opportunity that you feel passionate about?

◇ What natural abilities do you have that will help you with this ministry?

◇ Based on whether you're outgoing or reserved, what role can you see yourself playing in this ministry?

◇ Are there any experiences that you have had that make you especially qualified to help in this ministry?

EVANGELISM: SHARING Your Story and God's Story

[goal: to consider how the truths from this lesson might be applied to relationships with unbelievers]

Are there any opportunities within your church or youth ministry where an unbeliever can serve? If so, which ones? If not, why do you think that is?

📺 How might an unbeliever's service lead him or her closer to a relationship with God?

At the beginning of small groups such as this one, you should decide whether your group is open to inviting friends to join. If your group is open, list who you would like to invite and make plans for talking with them. Your small group leader or your leadership team may have already determined the group is closed at this time. If so, a good group respects and follows that decision. You may be able to invite friends to join you in the next LIFETOGETHER book.

Read How to Keep Your Small Group from Becoming a Clique (page 100) when you're at home.

WORSHIP: SURRENDERING Your Life to Honor God

[[goal: to focus on God's presence]

Some people refer to the church in sports terms when they say that most people in the church are spectators rather than players. The bleachers (pews) are filled with people watching the few who actually play (those who serve). Is that true at your church? Is that true of you?

For the next several sessions, you'll be challenged to get out of the bleachers and into the game by developing a heart for service. As you do this, take time to focus on God's presence through prayer so you can sense his leading in your life.

Share one specific way the others in the group can pray for you. This is a time to write down prayer requests in the **Prayer Request Log** (page 132).

Spend time thanking God for the people in your group and for the unique qualities each person has, which will lead to different acts of service and make your church stronger.

Before your group breaks, read **At Home This Week** together. (If everyone in the group has already done this in another LifeTogether book, you can skip the introduction if you'd like.)

You'll find three prayer resources in the back of the book. By reading and discussing them, you'll find your group prayer time more rewarding.

- 📖 Praying in Your Small Group (page 126). Read this on your own before the next session.
- 📖 Prayer Request Guidelines (page 128). Read and discuss these guidelines as a group.
- 📖 Prayer Options (page 130). Refer to this list for ideas to give your prayer time variety.

AT HOME THIS WEEK

Each week, you'll have at least four options to help you grow and learn on your own—which means you'll have more to contribute when you return to the group.

Daily Bible Readings

On page 112 you'll find **Daily Bible Readings,** a chart of Bible passages that correspond with the lessons—five for each week. If you choose this option, read one passage each day. Highlight it in your Bible, reflect on it, journal about it, or repeat it out loud as a prayer. You're free to interact with the Bible verses any way you want, just be sure to read God's love letter—the Bible. You'll find helpful tips in **How to Study the Bible** (page 113).

Memory Verses

Memorizing Bible verses is an important habit to develop as you learn to grow spiritually on your own. **Memory Verses** (page 116) lists six verses—one per week—for you to memorize if you want to plant God's Word in your heart. Memorizing verses (and making them stick for more than a few minutes) isn't easy, but the benefits are undeniable. You'll have God's Word with you wherever you go.

Journaling

You'll find blank pages for journaling beginning on page 121. At the end of each session, you'll find several options and a question or two to get your thoughts going—but you aren't limited to the ideas in this book. Use these pages to reflect, to write a letter to God, to note what you're learning, to compose a prayer, to ask a question, to draw a picture of your praise, to record your thoughts. For more suggestions about journaling, turn to **Journaling: Snapshots of Your Heart** (page 118).

If you'd like to choose journaling this week, respond to this question: *What's my biggest fear about getting involved in a ministry to serve God?*

Wrap It Up

Write out your answers to the session questions your group didn't have time to discuss.

This week share with the others in your group which option seems most appealing to try during the coming week. The variety of preferences is another reminder of how different the people in your group are.

During other weeks, take time to share with the group what you did **At Home This Week**.

LEARN A LITTLE MORE

Wonderfully made

Maybe you feel you're no longer a masterpiece because of the sin that's in your life. You've made bad choices, and others have hurt you. Sin has left its mark on who you are now, and you feel like a stained masterpiece. You may find it easier to see the stains than the masterpiece, but the stains don't erase your value. God wants you to change your focus. God will use even the stains from your past to restore the masterpiece to greater glory. You'll need to discover the uniqueness God created in you and express it through your life and service.

Written in your book

Several times throughout Scripture there is mention of a book (or scroll) that belongs to the Lord. In Psalm 56:8 God's complete knowledge of the psalmist's sorrow is written on a scroll. The prophet Malachi speaks of a scroll of remembrance that records the names of those who fear the Lord (3:16). Perhaps the most popular term is the "book of life," which contains the names of the faithful (Psalm 69:28; Revelation 20:15).

FOR FURTHER STUDY

Genesis 1:27
Job 31:4
Matthew 6:26

NOTES

NOTES

WANNA BE GREAT? SERVE!

One of my favorite Christmas characters is Ebenezer Scrooge (For those of you visiting Earth for the first time, he's the main character in the book and movie *A Christmas Carol.)* One of the reasons I like him is because he has a first and last name that are fun to say. (Go ahead. Say them out loud. See what I mean?). But I also like Ebenezer Scrooge because of what he ultimately discovers about the joy of serving others. His entire life and reason for living is transformed the moment he chooses to stop being a vicious, mean-spirited boss and become a gracious man finding delight through serving others. It's a great story!

Ebenezer's amazing change is like the change people experience when God's Spirit transforms them. They move from selfish to servant. This change happens to those who allow God's purpose of ministry to infuse their lives and give them power to do what's unnatural—serve others rather than themselves.

Jesus modeled servanthood, he talked about it with his closest followers, and he challenged others to change their hearts and their ways. Not everyone took Jesus' words to heart. One day, a rich young ruler came to Jesus. He missed out on the greatest joy because he chose self over service. (If you want to read the conversation yourself, you'll find it in Matthew 19:16-22. It's worth reading on your own later). Fortunately, not all examples in the Bible were as clueless as this guy was rich.

The men and women who made up the early church and followed God's ways understood that Christianity included serving one another (Acts 2:44-47). Christians shared all that they had. They sold their possessions to help the poor. They cared for one another, and they discovered that their selfless actions met with God's favor. God blessed their servant hearts.

God continues to bless servants today. When you serve you'll find that you can't out-give or out-serve God. Serving others is not something you'll master right away. I battle the choices to serve others or myself every day of my life. I know which action God rewards, but it's tough to do what's right and serve when in my heart I'm so selfish.

In this lesson, you'll discuss what it means to have a servant's heart. Encourage and challenge each other as you prepare to grow as followers of Christ in ministry-mindedness. Spiritual maturity isn't easy or natural, and you'll need support from each other to make serving a regular part of your life.

FELLOWSHIP: CONNECTING Your Heart to Others'

Share about a time when you did something for someone without being asked.
- How did the person react?
- How did that reaction make you feel?
- What type of personal sacrifice was involved?

For many people, serving others isn't convenient and doesn't come naturally. How is it for you?

DISCIPLESHIP: GROWING to Be Like Jesus

Everyone has the drive to accomplish something in life. Jesus knew the secret to true greatness. When he taught his disciples, he turned their entire understanding of life upside down. His ideas weren't just clever or profound; they radically changed everything about what it means to pursue greatness and become great.

42Jesus called them together and said, "You know that those who are regarded as rulers of the Gentiles lord it over them, and their high officials exercise authority over them. 43Not so with you. Instead, whoever wants to become great among you must be your servant, 44and whoever wants to be first must be slave of all. 45For even the Son of Man did not come to be served, but to serve, and to give his life as a ransom for many."

—Mark 10:42-45

Jesus makes a strong distinction between the world's way and God's way. Why is the world the way it is?
- Why are most people eager to have power?

Is there something wrong with exercising authority? Did Jesus mean we should get rid of all forms of authority? Explain why you think so.

4

What does it mean to be great in the eyes of the world?
 How does people know when they've achieved greatness?

5

What does it take to be great in God's eyes?
 Can you imagine yourself becoming great in this way? What will be difficult about it?

6

How was Jesus the perfect example of servanthood?

7

Respond to this statement: **Christians love talking about being a servant until someone treats them like one.**
 What do you like about this statement?
 What don't you like?

8

Slave is a pretty strong word that Jesus uses to describe the Christian life. Would **slave** be a good description of your commitment to serve God and others? Why or why not?

9

Jesus showed with his life what he meant by serving.
The apostle Paul explained serving like this:

¹If you have any encouragement from being united with Christ, if any comfort from his love, if any fellowship with the Spirit, if any tenderness and compassion, ²then make my joy complete by being like-minded, having the same love, being one in spirit and purpose. ³Do nothing out of selfish ambition or vain conceit, but in humility consider others better than yourselves. ⁴Each of you should look not only to your own interests, but also to the interests of others.
⁵Your attitude should be the same as that of Christ Jesus:

⁶Who, being in very nature God,
did not consider equality with God something to be grasped,
⁷but made himself nothing,
taking the very nature of a servant,
being made in human likeness.
⁸And being found in appearance as a man,
he humbled himself
and became obedient to death—even death on a cross!
—Philippians 2:1-8

Why does Paul begin this passage with these four questions? What point is he trying to make?

Define **selfish ambition** and **vain conceit** in your own words.

According to this passage, how was Jesus humble?

Respond to this statement: **Jesus never asks us to do something he didn't first do himself; we'll never have to serve more than he did.**
📖 What do you like about this? What don't you like?

SERVING others in love

MINISTRY: SERVING Others in Love

Ministry is all about serving God by serving others with an attitude of love. Jesus made it clear that when we serve others, we are serving him.

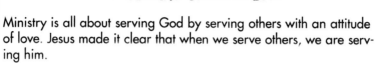

> **"The King will reply, 'I tell you the truth, whatever you did for one of the least of these brothers of mine, you did for me.' "**
>
> —Matthew 25:40

What are some practical ways you can serve others this week? Write your specific actions below.

Where?	Who?	When?	How?
At school			
At home			
In my small group			
At work			
At church			

The **Spiritual Health Assessment** (on pages 103–111) is a tool created to help you identify the state of your heart in various areas of your life. Take a few minutes to rate yourself in the Ministry section of the assessment. (You won't have to share your scores with the group.)

If you've never taken the Spiritual Health Assessment, consider taking the time to complete the remaining four areas later this week.

EVANGELISM: SHARING Your Story and God's Story

A strong step toward being evangelistic is serving those who don't have a relationship with God. Many unbelievers don't care about God's ways until they see you doing things that bring attention to the uniqueness of being a follower of Jesus. The apostle Paul said,

"...because our gospel came to you not simply with words, but also with power, with the Holy Spirit and with deep conviction. You know how we lived among you for your sake."

—1 Thessalonians 1:5

Why are words not as important as actions?

16

How can you serve those who don't know Christ?

17

Write a 30-day goal for how you can become a better servant to those who don't know God.
📖 Break into pairs and share your goals.

18

For the rest of the weeks your group is working through this book, let this person be your spiritual partner. Whenever your group breaks into pairs again, get together with your spiritual partner.

It's a normal part of group life to have a closer connection with some people than with others. If you find this to be the case and you'd like to spend more time throughout the week talking about life and challenging one another spiritually, consider using the **Accountability Questions** on page 102.

> Here's an antidote to any type of fear (which most of us experience when it comes to evangelism): Start with what's possible.

Don't begin with the scariest step in your goal. As you move out in faith to serve others, you'll experience positive responses that will help you move past some frightening steps in your goal.

If there's nothing about your goal that scares you, maybe it's too superficial. Your goal should be challenging.

As you serve others, don't make a show of being a servant. Read Matthew 6:2-4 and keep it tucked away in your heart. Jesus is speaking.

> **"So when you give to the needy, do not announce it with trumpets, as the hypocrites do in the synagogues and on the streets, to be honored by men. I tell you the truth, they have received their reward in full. But when you give to the needy, do not let your left hand know what your right hand is doing, so that your giving may be in secret. Then your Father, who sees what is done in secret, will reward you."**

WORSHIP: SURRENDERING Your Life to Honor God

Serving others can be frightening. You run the risk of the other person feeling better than you and looking down on you. Often, this fear keeps people from serving. It's too bad, because if a person thinks less of you because you serve—that's his loss, not yours. Besides, you're serving God when you're serving others.

Close your time together in prayer. Take time to surrender to God your desires to please yourself. Ask him to help you develop a servant's heart and to put you in situations where you'll be able to serve.

AT HOME THIS WEEK

Daily Bible Readings
Check out the Scriptures on page 112.

Memory Verses

Try memorizing a verse from page 116.

Journaling

Use **SCRIBBLE** pages, 121-125

📓 Write whatever is on your mind.

📓 Read your journal entry from last week and write a reflection on it.

📓 Respond to these questions: *Who do you know who lives with a servant's heart? What's different about this person? What needs to happen to your heart for you to become more of a servant?*

Wrap It Up

Write out your answers to the session questions your group didn't have time to discuss.

LEARN A LITTLE MORE

Gentiles

A Gentile is a person who wasn't born Jewish. Because the Jews were the chosen people of God (read about the life of Abraham in Genesis 12), Jews commonly viewed foreigners as second-class citizens—spiritually impaired. (Gentiles didn't receive God's law, so they couldn't worship God as the Jews could.) In the early church, there was conflict between the Jewish Christians and the Gentile Christians as they struggled to live out the commands Christ taught when the Jews felt superior. The truth is that our salvation isn't based on race.

Slave

Jesus used drastic language here. A slave is considered another person's property. Slaves did the lowliest work during Roman times. It isn't likely that Jesus means we should act as though other people own us; in fact, God owns us. (See 1 Corinthians 6:19-20.) More likely, Jesus means we should freely choose the kind of lowly service that proud people would leave for slaves to do. Jesus is not advising us to let others dominate and control us. Jesus himself served constantly but never let others control him. We need a strong awareness of our true Master if we want to choose lowly service without being controlled by people.

Son of Man

This term was Jesus' favorite title for himself; he used it more than 80 times in the gospels. This title is significant for the following reasons:

- Jesus was fully divine (the Son of God), and he was also fully human.
- His nationality was Jewish, but he is a representative of all people (that is, he didn't refer to himself as the Son of Abraham).
- The term *son of man* originated in the Old Testament (see Daniel 7:13-14), where it was used in reference to the promised Messiah. By using this title Jesus was announcing that he was the Messiah.

FOR FURTHER STUDY

John 13:1-20
Matthew 11:7-19
Romans 12:9-21

NOTES

CONGRATULATIONS! YOU'RE GIFTED!

One time I was trying to explain to my small group about God's unique distribution of spiritual gifts. This is not an easy concept to understand, let alone explain. So here's what I did. I gave each guy a wrapped gift. I told them we were going to open them one at a time. I also told them that they had to share their gifts with others or their gifts would be incomplete. Their confusion over the initial instructions was matched by their excitement about receiving gifts.

The first person ripped open his wrapping paper to discover a large brown plastic potato shape. With a disappointed look, he then watched (with confusion) the next person unwrap his gift. As each student took a turn unwrapping gifts they were puzzled at how unique and unusual they were; an ear, a pair of rubber eyes, a plastic nose, lips, ears…all the parts of Mr. Potato Head. Needless to say, none of the guys thanked me. Okay, so it was a lame idea.

This unusual gift exchange was my attempt to teach the guys about spiritual gifts. Much like my creative lesson, spiritual gifts are confusing yet exciting to possess. According to God's Word, Christians receive gifts from God (called spiritual gifts) to use in serving others and building up the church. No believer receives all the spiritual gifts but every believer is gifted with at least one. Who gets which gift and how many is up to God's distribution plans.

Unfortunately many Christians go their entire lives without ever recognizing and developing their spiritual gifts. Many people rely on their natural abilities and don't pursue the discovery of their spiritual gifts. During this session, I want to be sure you're aware that you're gifted by God. Your small group time won't produce all the answers about how God has gifted you, but it will help you become aware of the spiritual gifts in the Bible, get you thinking about how God uses gifts, and help you consider the differences between spiritual gifts and natural abilities. It's not an easy lesson, but you'll have plenty to discuss. Natural abilities are great but when added to your spiritual gifts, watch out! Serving God gets exciting!

FELLOWSHIP: CONNECTING Your Heart to Others'

What are some of your natural abilities? List three things you think you're pretty good at. (You're not bragging by listing strengths. It's okay to be good at some things.)

DISCIPLESHIP: GROWING to Be Like Jesus

One of my favorite things to say to people is, "Congratulations, you're gifted!" I love to celebrate with others when they learn that God has gifted them with awesome potential to make an eternal difference for him. In a few moments, you're going to study a classic passage about spiritual gifts. I don't know about you, but I often don't feel like I'm good enough to be used by God. I have a hard time believing God would choose to work through me. But the great thing is that God wants to use anyone and everyone to make a difference in this world!

4There are different kinds of gifts, but the same Spirit. 5There are different kinds of service, but the same Lord. 6There are different kinds of working, but the same God works all of them in all men.
7Now to each one the manifestation of the Spirit is given for the common good...
14Now the body is not made up of one part but of many. 15If the foot should say, "Because I am not a hand, I do not belong to the body," it would not for that reason cease to be part of the body. 16And if the ear should say, "Because I am not an eye, I do not belong to the body," it would not for that reason cease to be part of the body. 17If the whole body were an eye, where would the sense of hearing be? If the whole body were an ear, where would the sense of smell be? 18But in fact God has arranged the parts in the body, every one of them, just as he wanted them to be. 19If they were all one part, where would the body be? 20As it is, there are many parts, but one body. 21The eye cannot say to the hand, "I don't need

you!" And the head cannot say to the feet, "I don't need you!" [22]On the contrary, those parts of the body that seem to be weaker are indispensable, [23]and the parts that we think are less honorable we treat with special honor. And the parts that are unpresentable are treated with special modesty, [24]while our presentable parts need no special treatment. But God has combined the members of the body and has given greater honor to the parts that lacked it, [25]so that there should be no division in the body, but that its parts should have equal concern for each other. [26]If one part suffers, every part suffers with it; if one part is honored, every part rejoices with it.

—1 Corinthians 12:4-7, 14-26

Why is it important that, although there are different kinds of gifts and service, there is only one Spirit, only one Lord?

Is equality something Christians struggle with? Does the church have a problem with some people believing they are better than others? Explain why you think so.

Three times in verses 4–6 Paul repeats that all spiritual gifts and all acts of true service come from the same Spirit of God. Why do you suppose he makes such a big deal about this?

What does Paul mean by the body? What's his point in using this metaphor? What are some clues from the text that support your answer?

Respond to this statement: **There is both great unity and great diversity in the church, and many Christians often act as if neither is true.**

➤ What do you like about it? What don't you like?

7

Different body parts—eye, ear, foot—are mentioned in this passage. What is Paul referring to when he uses these examples? Be as specific as you can.

8

Reread verses 18–19. Why does God use different parts to accomplish his will? Why not create everyone the same and use them as he chooses?

9

Respond to this statement: **Since the parts are different from one another, some must also be more important than the others.**

➤ What do you like about it? What don't you like?

10

Give an example of an individual Christian doing something that impacts the entire body of Christ.

11

Paul wrote this passage to deal with specific problems the church in Corinth was facing. Based on this passage, what might some of those problems have been?

MINISTRY: SERVING Others in Love

In sessions 1 and 2, you discussed how God created you as his unique masterpiece and calls you to serve others. In this session you're learning about spiritual gifts and natural abilities.

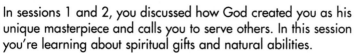

During the ministry segment you'll discuss spiritual gifts and during the evangelism segment you'll talk about natural abilities.

When it comes to understanding spiritual gifts, four primary Bible passages reveal specific spiritual gifts: Romans 12:3-8; 1 Corinthians 12:1-11, 27-31; Ephesians 4:11-12; and 1 Peter 4:9-11. It would be wise to do a more complete study of spiritual gifts than you have time for during this one small group session. During this session you're being exposed to the spiritual gifts but not determining exactly what your spiritual gifts are. You'll have to discover your gifts through serving, getting feedback from friends, and discerning how you feel as you serve.

One of the ways to learn how God has designed you to serve others is by discovering your unique S.H.A.P.E. The following S.H.A.P.E. acrostic is a tool I like to use to help Christians better understand how God can use several aspects of their lives to serve him. Over your next few meetings you'll look at the following five signs to help you better see God's design for you.

Spiritual gifts	Session 3
Heart	Session 6
Abilities	Session 3
Personality	Session 4
Experiences	Session 5

Turn to **Spiritual Gifts** (pages 81–90). On a scale of 1 to 10, rate your response to each statement. You can then estimate your overall rating for each spiritual gift, or if you prefer to be precise, you can total your ratings for the questions in each section and divide by the number of statements.

12

Some Bible teachers refer to a shorter list of spiritual gifts, and others might argue for additional gifts. Regardless of the exact number, the gifts listed will help you begin to discover your spiritual gifts.

Transfer your overall rating for each spiritual gift to **Finding Your S.H.A.P.E.: Spiritual Gifts** (page 91), and put a star next to the three spiritual gifts that received your highest scores. The scores don't mean that you have the particular spiritual gift. It merely indicates the possibility. You can pursue ministry opportunities that would be likely to use those gifts.

Share with the group one spiritual gift that you may have that surprised you.

 # EVANGELISM: SHARING Your Story and God's Story

How might your strongest natural abilities (see your list on page 42, Fellowship, question 1) become an aid to your evangelism?

Turn to **Finding Your S.H.A.P.E.: Heart and Abilities** (page 91) and place check marks next to the abilities you believe you have. Be sure to add any natural abilities you think you have that aren't listed there.

 # WORSHIP: SURRENDERING Your Life to Honor God

When you were a little child you probably played games that required someone to surrender. In the last moment of the game you'd say, "I give up." It was a way of saying, "I surrender because I know I can't win." In childhood games, giving up is considered a decision of weakness, but spiritually, surrender is a sign of strength.

It's natural to use your gifts to get what you want, to serve yourselves. As you discuss living a life of surrender, you must also submit your abilities and spiritual gifts to God and be willing to use them according to his purposes.

Make a commitment to one another that you'll do your best to learn more about spiritual gifts and put yourself in serving opportunities where you can exercise them. Also make a commitment to one another that you'll look for opportunities to encourage—and therefore confirm—one another's natural abilities and spiritual gifts.

Close your group time by thanking God for loving you enough to gift you. Ask him to help you discover your spiritual gifts and to give you the power to use your natural abilities for his glory.

AT HOME THIS WEEK

Daily Bible Readings
Check out the Scriptures on page 112.

Memory Verses
Try memorizing a verse from page 116.

Journaling
Use **SCRIBBLE** pages, 121-125
📖 Write whatever is on your mind.
📖 Read your journal entry from last week and write a reflection on it.
📖 Respond to these questions: *How did this session help me toward the 30-day goal I wrote in session 2? Based on what I learned, do I need to adjust my goal?*

Wrap It Up
Write out your answers to the session questions your group didn't have time to discuss.

LEARN A LITTLE MORE

Gifts
People are born with some abilities and develop their skills through practice, but

they receive spiritual gifts from the Holy Spirit. Once given, spiritual gifts usually need to be developed through practice.

Common good
Spiritual gifts are not given to puff up our egos or to win people's attention or respect. They're for the good of others—to build up the whole Christian community.

Now the body is not made up of one part but of many
The community of faith in Christ is at the same time unified and diverse. Great problems arise when either one is emphasized to the exclusion of the other. With too much unity, every believer becomes a carbon copy. Every believer learns the same way, worships the same way, serves the same way, and grows the same way. Individual passion is ignored, and the vibrancy of the church suffers. With too much diversity, the individuals become more important than the community. This often translates into some individuals becoming more important than the whole.

Finding the balance between these two is difficult. We can be thankful that the church is not left to manage itself. We have the direction and power of the Holy Spirit. If every believer makes it his or her business to serve others in love, we'll be able to overcome any mistakes we may make.

God has arranged the parts in the body, every one of them, just as he wanted them to be
We know God is the Big Boss, and he has decided how things ought to be. The big churchy words for this concept are sovereignty and providence. Our responsibility is not to rearrange what God has determined, but to humbly accept his ordering of things. It is true that there is sin in this world, and many things fall short of the way they ought to be. It's also true that some of us would disagree with God and argue with the way he has arranged things.

FOR FURTHER STUDY

Romans 12:1-8
1 Peter 4:10-11
Ephesians 4:11-13

NOTES

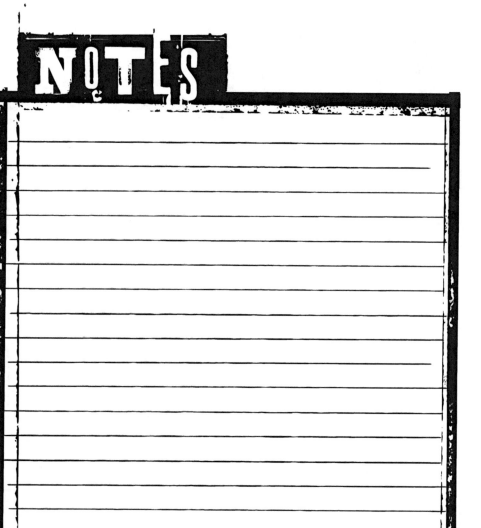

If you are watching the LIFETOGETHER DVD, you may use this page to take notes.

NOTES

If you are watching the LIFETOGETHER DVD, you may use this page to take notes.

YOUR UNIQUE PERSONALITY

Many years ago I learned a painful truth: My personality isn't the best personality. I hate to admit it, but I used to think that if people didn't have a personality like mine, they weren't as good as me. I actually believed that the most powerful and contagious Christians were the ones who had outgoing personalities, loved to be around people, and could talk to everyone in the room. I believed this until I met a hot-looking, quiet, reserved, gentle young lady. Even though her personality is the exact opposite of mine, I fell in love with her and we married.

While we were dating, Cathy and I helped in our church junior high group. We were still teenagers ourselves. I was the type who was friendly to everyone and knew the names of everyone in the room. While I was "working the room," Cathy was standing in the corner talking with one girl. She wasn't good at meeting a lot of people and didn't go out of her way to make conversation. At first, I was bothered at how little she seemed to care about the health of our youth ministry.

One time, after youth group, I pushed a little too hard when I said (with an accusing tone), "How many people did *you* talk to tonight?"

She calmly said, "Two or three."

I shot back quickly, "I talked to that many people in the first minute." As the idiot I was, I wanted to make the point that she needed to be more like me if she wanted to be good at ministry.

She didn't appreciate my obnoxious approach and calmly asked, "How many people did you talk to tonight about Jesus?"

Ouch. I was down for the count. I had no response, and I felt shame. I talked to everyone in the room on a surface level while she spoke to a few and went deep in those conversations.

That night I learned a great lesson. Different personalities impact how people do ministry and one type is not better than another. God uses people in different ways. Today, over 20 years later, we still minister together; only I've learned how our personality differences work to complement each other.

Your personality is a great one! Don't try to be someone else, and don't *try* to make others like you. Your personality will affect how you serve God. God's design is perfect. If you're like me, it may take a while to figure out what his design is and how he's going to use it, so you'd better get talking with your small group members!

FELLOWSHIP: CONNECTING Your Heart to Others'

How do you define personality?

Share which type of personality you relate to most: the outgoing one who likes to talk with everyone or the reserved one who enjoys deeper conversations with a few.

DISCIPLESHIP: GROWING to Be Like Jesus

If you were to paint a picture of all the different personalities of the people in the Bible, you'd find many unique types of people. There is, of course, no single personality that's better than another. Different doesn't translate into more important! In this session, we're going to look at two different personalities God used to make a difference for his kingdom.

13For you have heard of my previous way of life in Judaism, how intensely I persecuted the church of God and tried to destroy it. I was advancing in Judaism beyond many Jews of my own age and was extremely zealous for the traditions of my fathers. But when God, who set me apart from birth and called me by his grace, was pleased to reveal his Son in me so that I might preach him among the Gentiles, I did not consult any man, nor did I go up to Jerusalem to see those who were apostles before I was, but I went immediately into Arabia and later returned to Damascus.

—Galatians 1:13-17

What do you learn directly or indirectly about Paul's personality from this passage?

What traits did Paul have that could have been either positive or negative, depending on how well he surrendered them to God?

Who do you know with a personality similar to Paul's? What do you like about that personality type? What do you dislike about it?

[1] Six days before the Passover, Jesus arrived at Bethany, where Lazarus lived, whom Jesus had raised from the dead. Here a dinner was given in Jesus' honor. Martha served, while Lazarus was among those reclining at the table with him. Then Mary took about a pint of pure nard, an expensive perfume; she poured it on Jesus' feet and wiped his feet with her hair. And the house was filled with the fragrance of the perfume.

But one of his disciples, Judas Iscariot, who was later to betray him, objected, "Why wasn't this perfume sold and the money given to the poor? It was worth a year's wages." He did not say this because he cared about the poor but because he was a thief; as keeper of the money bag, he used to help himself to what was put into it.

"Leave her alone," Jesus replied. "It was intended that she should save this perfume for the day of my burial. You will always have the poor among you, but you will not always have me."

—John 12:1-8

What do you learn directly and indirectly about Mary's personality from this passage?

There is no historical record that Mary traveled anywhere to preach the gospel. What value can a personality like hers have in the church?

8 Mary's actions were misunderstood, and she did not explain her own actions. Instead, Jesus was her advocate. Why is it easy to misunderstand other people?

9 What are some personality types that are difficult for you to get along with?

10 What does it say about God that he created people like Paul as well as people like Mary?

11 How might your personality impact the way you serve?

12 What types of ministry opportunities might be good for people who are outgoing that wouldn't be good for people who are reserved?

13 What types of ministry opportunities might be good for people who are reserved that wouldn't be good for people who are outgoing?

MINISTRY: SERVING Others in Love

Remember S.H.A.P.E., which was introduced during the last session? Turn to **Finding Your S.H.A.P.E.: Personality** on page 92. Take the time to answer the questions (on your own if you don't have enough time during the small group session), which will help you consider four aspects of your personality:

- What you're like around other people

- How you make decisions

- What you're like in your relationships with others

- How you use your time

There aren't right and wrong answers. The right personality is *your* personality. Your answers may help you discover what ministry opportunities might be best suited for your S.H.A.P.E.

The goal isn't to see if you have the "correct" or "best" personality. What's important is if you're aware of the uniqueness God has placed within you and if your personality is influencing how you serve him. When you better understand your personality, you'll be free of guilt or negative feelings about competing or comparing yourself with others.

Share your results with the group. How do others see you?

How might your personality impact your ministry choice?

EVANGELISM: SHARING Your Story and God's Story

When I was in high school, I drove a small car that could fit four friends comfortably. Every week my goal was to cram as many friends as I could into my car and take them to church. Comfort wasn't an issue. The more people in the car, the happier I was. I never wanted to show up at church without unbelieving friends.

When my wife, Cathy, was in high school she would bring a couple of really good friends to church. She didn't invite the whole school like I tried to do. Rather she focused on her best friends.

God uses both types of personalities in his plan to reach those without the good news.

How does your personality impact your evangelistic efforts? (Try to focus specifically on your personality, not on other issues like your fears or your spiritual condition.)

17

WORSHIP: SURRENDERING Your Life to Honor God

What aspects of your personality are you thankful for? Take time to share a few.

18

Ask God to help you find ways to serve him that best fit your personality.

19

AT HOME THIS WEEK

Daily Bible Readings
Check out the scriptures on page 112.

Memory Verses
Try memorizing a verse from page 116.

Journaling
Use **SCRIBBLE** pages, 121-125
- Write whatever is on your mind.
- Read your journal entry from last week and write a reflection on it.
- Respond to this question: *What did I learn about myself from this session?*

Wrap It Up
Write out your answers to the session questions your group didn't have time to discuss.

LEARN A LITTLE MORE

I persecuted the church
In the beginning, the early church was considered a renegade Jewish movement. Jesus was Jewish, as were his disciples, yet his teachings were not accepted by all Jewish leaders. The book of Acts records the persecution the first Christians faced. Before he learned the truth, Paul was active in persecuting Christians.

Passover
The Passover was a seven-day celebration commemorating God's deliverance of the Israelites from captivity in Egypt. This was an important holiday for the Jews and early Christians. Jesus redefined the meaning of Passover through his death on the cross, saving all of humanity from slavery to sin.

Wiped his feet with her hair
Mary had to get down on her hands and knees to get so close to Jesus' feet. For a woman to unbind her hair in public was shocking in that culture and put Mary's reputation at risk. Mary's action was a bold one that expressed her attitude of humility. Serving others can also require risk and humility.

FOR FURTHER STUDY

Philippians 2:1-4; 3:4-14
Luke 7:47
John 13:1-20

NOTES

SERVING FROM EXPERIENCE

Crisis hit my family when my dad passed away. The crisis wasn't that he died; it was the pain from missing him so much. The last few months of his life, I begged God to either heal him or take him to heaven so his suffering would end. But when Dad's pain was over, my emotional pain intensified. I couldn't believe the strength of my feelings. The intensity of the loss took me by surprise. As a minister, I had presided over several funerals, but this one was different...it was *my* dad.

I found comfort from an unexpected person—a teenager named Diego. One day at church Diego said, "I know what you're going through. My dad died last year, and it really hurts. I realize that I'm only 14 and you're old"—that hurt a little—"but if you need to talk, I'd love to listen." I took him up on his offer, and we talked about our dads, grief, heaven, death, missing a loved one, and the gift of life.

When my father died, I received over 100 phone calls and letters from friends and church members, but the simple offer from Diego is the one I'll always cherish. He had experienced what I had and was God's messenger to me when I needed help.

I have a friend who is dying of Amyotrophic Lateral Sclerosis (ALS, also known as Lou Gehrig's disease). I was with him recently, and I was able to comfort the family. I don't know anything about ALS, but I now know about death. I know how it feels to lose someone you love. Before my dad died, I talked about death philosophically, now I talk about it experientially. Last night, I was Diego to this grieving family. I was able to do for them what a 14-year-old did for me. That's how it works. God uses our experiences—both good and bad—to help us as we help others.

Like your personality, your experiences help shape who you are. Don't be embarrassed about your past hurts. God won't waste them. Your hurts can bring healing, hope and help to others. And what a gift your experiences can be to others. (Thanks again, Diego!)

FELLOWSHIP: CONNECTING Your Heart to Others'

On the timeline below, write your birth date and today's date.

birth date   today's date

Mark the points that represent significant experiences in
your life and draw a symbol for each one. Include positive
and negative experiences. Here are some examples

- Won the championship
- Ruined my art collection
- Hiked across three states with Dad
- Moved to a new city

- My parents divorced
- I accidentally started a kitchen fire
  while cooking French fries
- I got serious about Jesus

You won't be able to include every significant
event in your life but include at least five or six.

Briefly share your timeline with others in your group.

DISCIPLESHIP: GROWING to Be Like Jesus

In this session we're going to take a long look at the life of Peter,
one of the 12 disciples. Peter was typically the most vocal one of
the group, and he sometimes said things he probably regretted
later. Yet God used some of his tough experiences to turn him into a
great leader in the early church.

**Simon Peter asked him, "Lord, where are you
going?"**
   **Jesus replied, "Where I am going, you cannot
follow now, but you will follow later."**
   **Peter asked, "Lord, why can't I follow you now?
I will lay down my life for you."**
   **Then Jesus answered, "Will you really lay down
your life for me? I tell you the truth, before the
rooster crows, you will disown me three times!"**
                                                    —John 13:36-38

4 If you were Peter, how do you think you would have responded to Jesus?

Jesus was arrested a few hours after this conversation, and Peter ran away with the other disciples. Peter hid in a nearby courtyard while Jesus was being questioned. What do you imagine Peter must have been feeling?

Then the detachment of soldiers with its commander and the Jewish officials arrested Jesus. They bound him and brought him first to Annas, who was the father-in-law of Caiaphas, the high priest that year. Caiaphas was the one who had advised the Jews that it would be good if one man died for the people.

Simon Peter and another disciple were following Jesus. Because this disciple was known to the high priest, he went with Jesus into the high priest's courtyard, but Peter had to wait outside at the door. The other disciple, who was known to the high priest, came back, spoke to the girl on duty there and brought Peter in.

"You are not one of his disciples, are you?" the girl at the door asked Peter.

He replied, "I am not."

It was cold, and the servants and officials stood around a fire they had made to keep warm. Peter also was standing with them, warming himself.

Meanwhile, the high priest questioned Jesus about his disciples and his teaching...

As Simon Peter stood warming himself, he was asked, "You are not one of his disciples, are you?"

He denied it, saying, "I am not."

One of the high priest's servants, a relative of the man whose ear Peter had cut off, challenged him, "Didn't I see you with him in the olive grove?" Again Peter denied it, and at that moment a rooster began to crow.

—John 18:12-19, 25-27

6 Why do you think Peter denied Jesus, even though Jesus had told Peter what was going to happen?

7 How do you think Peter felt the moment he heard the rooster begin to crow?

8 How can our failures be turned into something good? How can God use them to make us more mature?

Jesus was crucified the same day Peter denied him. We know that's not the end of the story. Jesus defeated death and rose from the dead. Before he went into heaven, Jesus spent time with his disciples:

When they had finished eating, Jesus said to Simon Peter, "Simon son of John, do you truly love me more than these?"

"Yes, Lord," he said, "you know that I love you."

Jesus said, "Feed my lambs."

Again Jesus said, "Simon son of John, do you truly love me?"

He answered, "Yes, Lord, you know that I love you."

Jesus said, "Take care of my sheep."

The third time he said to him, "Simon son of John, do you love me?"

Peter was hurt because Jesus asked him the third time, "Do you love me?" He said, "Lord, you know all things; you know that I love you."

Jesus said, "Feed my sheep. I tell you the truth, when you were younger you dressed yourself and went where you wanted; but when you are old you will stretch out your hands, and someone else will dress you and lead you where you do not want to go." Jesus said this to indicate the kind of death by which Peter would glorify God. Then he said to him, "Follow me!"

—John 21:15-19

9 Why did Jesus ask Peter the same question three times?

10 Who are the lambs and sheep that Jesus is referring to?

11 Do you think Peter felt disqualified to be used by Jesus? Explain your answer.

12 Jesus wanted to use Peter even though Peter had denied him. What kind of hope does this hold for you?

13 How might Peter have felt after this conversation with Jesus?

14 Why might Jesus have made the comparison between Peter's youth and old age?

MINISTRY: SERVING Others in Love

The events in Peter's life reveal to us that God can use broken and imperfect lives to make a difference in the world. Peter was a big-mouthed, cocky fisherman who became a wise and gentle leader. We can assume that some of his painful and positive experiences shaped his life and molded him as a minister. The same can happen to you.

Transfer your experiences from the timeline on page 60 (Fellowship question 1) to **Finding Your S.H.A.P.E.: Experiences** (page 95). If you remember additional experiences, write them down too.

With each experience there is most likely a lesson you've learned or an insight you've gained. Turn to **Finding Your S.H.A.P.E.: Experiences** (page 95) and write down the insight you've gained or the lesson you learned from the experience. You may need to come back to this later, because sometimes it takes a while before the lesson comes into focus.

EVANGELISM: SHARING Your Story and God's Story

Many of your past experiences can be used to share about Jesus with others.

Eleven-year-old Brandon is on my son's baseball team. He and his family told me that he was recently diagnosed with diabetes. They're struggling with the adjustments he has to make because of this disease. I initially felt helpless, because I didn't know what to say or how to comfort them.

Then I remembered Steven, a 16-year-old at my church who has had diabetes since he was a child. I connected the two families. Steven knew exactly what to say to Brandon: "It's tough, but with Christ's help it is possible." I could have used those words, but they wouldn't have been as powerful.

And Steven's parents were able to help Brandon's parents

understand what it's like to raise a son struggling with diabetes. Brandon and his family aren't believers yet, but because of Steven's concern and compassion they've started attending our church.

If it weren't for Steven's experience and willingness to share, I doubt they'd be attending our church. God isn't wasting Steven's painful experience. Actually, if Brandon's family places their faith in Jesus, Steven's disease will have had eternal benefits.

Which of your experiences can be used to share the hope of Jesus with a non-Christian person?

WORSHIP: SURRENDERING Your Life to Honor God

As you pray together, take a moment to thank God that he has a plan to use your experiences to minister to others.

AT HOME THIS WEEK

Daily Bible Readings
Check out the Scriptures on page 112.

Memory Verses
Try memorizing a verse from page 116.

Journaling
Use **SCRIBBLE** pages, 121-125
- Write whatever is on your mind.
- Read your journal entry from last week and write a reflection on it.
- Finish this statement: *My life experiences and lessons learned have made me a stronger person because I...*

Wrap It Up

Write out your answers to the session questions your group didn't have time to discuss.

LEARN A LITTLE MORE

Background: Why does God allow pain?

The truth is that God is not the author of pain. He loves us and wants nothing but the best for us. So why do crazy-painful things happen? Isn't God strong enough to make all the pain go away?

God *is* strong enough to make all pain go away, and some day he will. Until then we can rely on the Holy Spirit for strength, and we know God will do something good in our lives through our struggles.

Many people wonder why God even allowed sin and pain in the first place. This is a natural question to ask. Pain exists in the world because it's the *consequence* of bad decisions. God gave us the ability to choose because he loves us. He didn't create a world filled with robots unable to choose on their own.

Let's work through this one more time: God loves us, so he gave us the ability to choose whether we want to love him back. For a decision to be a real choice, it must have results—consequences. The consequences of bad decisions (choices that don't choose God's way) are pain and suffering.

Another disciple

Most people believe the other disciple was the author of this gospel, John the Apostle.

FOR FURTHER STUDY

Matthew 16:21-28; 17:1-5
John 21:15-22
Acts 2:14; 3:6, 16; 4:8-20

NOTES

NOTES

If you are watching the LIFETOGETHER DVD, you may use this page to take notes.

SERVING WITH PASSION

'I've never been excited to serve in our church's nursery. Even when my children were babies I had no desire to help there. Don't get me wrong. I love babies when they're mine or when they're visiting and will leave soon. When babies are near me, I like them. When they're gone, I love them. I wish I were spiritual enough to be passionate about handling, feeding, changing, and comforting the children who stink up our nursery, but I can't. I'm thankful many people at my church love these demons...uh...babies.

I have a God-given passion to serve teenagers. Just as I have uncomfortable feelings about babies, some adults would rather give birth through their nostrils than work with teenagers. But I love them! I can't see myself doing anything else. When I watch the lights go on for students spiritually and see the actions follow as they surrender their hearts to God's ways, I know I'm doing exactly what God created me to do. It's not my job—it's my passion!

During this session you'll be discussing what each of you are passionate about. God gave you passions! Certain activities or people in the world and the church will trigger excitement in you. When this passion mixes with the other areas of your S.H.A.P.E., you won't be able to imagine what life was like before you discovered God's unique design for you.

This is the last time you'll be meeting with this book as your guide, so make sure you're honest and be sure to challenge each another to get out of the bleachers and into the game. Ministry isn't easy, but when you're serving in an area that fits your S.H.A.P.E., you'll enjoy it! It's so exciting I could hold a baby...until he cries. Then I'm out of S.H.A.P.E.

FELLOWSHIP: CONNECTING Your Heart to Others'

One myth too many people believe goes like this: "Serving God will never be enjoyable. God wants you to step out of your comfort zone to do what is tough."

Following Jesus may be uncomfortable, but God's goal is not to make you miserable. He wants you to use your passion to discover where you can effectively minister.

What do you love to do? Think of sports, music, school, church, friends, family, recreation, and so forth.

What don't you do that you'd like to have the opportunity to do?

If you knew you could do any type of ministry and it would be successful, what would you like to try?

SERVING others in love

DISCIPLESHIP: GROWING to Be Like Jesus

No one can do everything that's important. It's impossible. There are too many causes, projects, and good things to be done. You have to choose so you can focus your efforts on what's most important.

God has created everyone uniquely, which means that your individual passions may not be shared by others. That's okay. At the core of who you are, at the center of your heart, you'll find your desires, motives, feelings, and attitudes. When you feel passionate about something God feels passionate about, then you have a strong clue that your passion is something you should pursue. What makes you weep? What injustice makes you angry? What gives you joy? What do you ache to see God accomplish in the world? Your life-long challenge is to serve in an area that taps into your heart's passion.

During this session, we're going to look at Paul's passion.

I want you to know how glad I am that it's me sitting here in this jail and not you. There's a lot of suffering to be entered into in this world—the kind of suffering Christ takes on. I welcome the chance to take my share in the church's part of that suffering. When I became a servant in this church, I experienced this suffering as a sheer gift, God's way of helping me serve you, laying out the whole truth.

This mystery has been kept in the dark for a long time, but now it's out in the open. God wanted everyone, not just Jews, to know this rich and glorious secret inside and out, regardless of their background, regardless of their religious standing. The mystery in a nutshell is just this: Christ is in you, therefore you can look forward to sharing in God's glory. It's that simple. That is the substance of our Message. We preach Christ, warning people not to add to the Message. We teach in a spirit of profound common sense so that we can bring each person to maturity. To be mature is to be basic. Christ! No more, no less. That's what I'm working so hard at day after day, year after year, doing my best with the energy God so generously gives me.

I want you to realize that I continue to work as hard as I know how for you, and also for the Christians over at Laodicea.

—Colossians 1:24-2:1 THE MESSAGE

4 Paul seems crazy to consider suffering as a "sheer gift." Why was he able to have this attitude? What enabled Paul to endure jail?

5 When you're doing what you love, is it easier for you to endure hardship? Explain why you think so.

6 After reading this passage, what do you think Paul was passionate about?

7 Are you as passionate about something as much as Paul is? Or does Paul's kind of passion seem like something you might never have? Explain your thoughts.

8 What is the mystery that Paul's talking about? Explain it in your own words.

9 Respond to this statement: **We always work harder when we do something we love.**
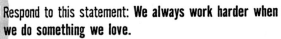 What do you like about it? What don't you like?

What does verse 28 mean: "so that we can bring each person to maturity"?

10

The same verse says, "To be mature is to be basic." Now that you're at the end of this book on serving, complete this sentence in your own words: To be mature is to...

11

12
Paul says that he's trying to do his best with the energy that God gave him. How are energy and passion alike? How are they different?
■ Will energy have anything to do with what you want to do to as you serve God?

MINISTRY: SERVING Others in Love

The apostle Paul was passionate about preaching and starting churches even when it meant being thrown in jail or killed. (He experienced both.) While most of us do not experience this level of passion, we do deeply care about specific issues, and we enjoy helping in areas where we feel a sense of passion.

Turn to **Finding Your S.H.A.P.E.: Heart and Abilities** on page 91. Circle the things you love to do. Rank your circled choices.

13

14
How might your areas of passion be useful in a ministry that you might start or join?

15 By now you should have completed **Finding Your S.H.A.P.E.** on pages 90–95. Don't be too concerned if you didn't have enough small group time to process the entire evaluation. You can come back to it on your own in the near future or your small group can schedule an additional session to dig into your discoveries a little deeper.

Based on what you've discovered about yourself so far, what ministry might you want to get involved in? How might you begin to develop your ministry during the next three months? **16**

Caution
You can easily get overloaded by serving in too many places. Try to limit your involvement to one or two ministries at a time until you discover the one that fits your unique S.H.A.P.E. the best.

Challenge
When trying new areas of ministry, plan to stay with it for a while. (Exactly how long depends on how often you participate. One to three months is a good minimum.) You want to build a reputation for being reliable, but you also want to give God time to work in you before determining whether you're a match for a particular ministry.

EVANGELISM: SHARING Your Story and God's Story

Passion is a key component to effective evangelism. All believers are called to share the gospel with others. However, God can give some people a unique love for individual people or groups. For example, God gave Paul a passion to preach to the Gentiles. He gave Peter a passion to preach to Jews. Nobel Peace Prize winner Mother Teresa was passionate about caring for the poor and sick in India. I have a passion to help teenagers. What about you?

An aid to being evangelistic is knowing the target of your passion. You may have a passion for helping children in foreign countries. Others may feel passionate about reaching their campus, their relatives, their neighborhood, their sports teams, and so on. One of my students collects shoes and gives them to homeless people. He's passionate about bringing Jesus to the inner city.

Are you passionate about reaching a certain group of people? If yes, who?

WORSHIP: SURRENDERING Your Life to Honor God

Over the last six small group meetings you have gathered a lot of information about yourself. You have also considered serving God in a ministry based on your unique S.H.A.P.E. Some in your small group may be overloaded and filled with fear while others are anxious to start serving in a ministry.

In these last moments of this session, thank God that he would use you in ministry. Appreciate him for designing you to serve him. When he made you, he knew exactly what S.H.A.P.E. you would need to serve him best.

> **Thank you for making me so wonderfully complex! Your workmanship is marvelous—and how well I know it.**
>
> —Psalm 139:14 NLT

End your time together by thanking God for what you've learned in this group. Also be sure to thank your leader for investing time with you.

WHAT'S NEXT?

Do you agree to continue meeting together? If yes, continue on with the remaining questions.

Five other books in the LifeTogether series help you establish God's purposes in your life. Discuss which topic your group will study next.

Starting to Go Where God Wants You to Be: 6 Small Group Sessions on Beginning Life Together
Connecting Your Heart to Others': 6 Small Group Sessions on Fellowship
Growing to Be Like Jesus: 6 Small Group Sessions on Discipleship
Sharing Your Story and God's Story: 6 Small Group Sessions on Evangelism
Surrendering Your Life to Honor God: 6 Small Group Sessions on Worship

Turn to the **Small Group Covenant** (page 96). Do you want to change anything in your covenant—time, date, shared values, and so on? Write down the changes you agree upon. (Transfer them into your next LifeTogether book.)

This is a good time to make suggestions for other chang-es—starting on time, paying attention when others are sharing, rotating leadership responsibilities, or whatever ideas you have—for improving the group.

AT HOME THIS WEEK

Daily Bible Readings
Check out the Scriptures on page 112.

Memory Verses
Try memorizing a verse from page 116.

Journaling
Use **SCRIBBLE** pages, 121-125
- Write whatever is on your mind.
- Read your journal entry from last week and write a reflection on it.
- Finish this sentence: *Based on my unique S.H.A.P.E., I'm ready to serve God. If I knew I wouldn't fail, I would serve him by...*

Wrap It Up
Write out your answers to the session questions your group didn't have time to discuss.

LEARN A LITTLE MORE

Suffering
Everyone on earth suffers. It's an inescapable part of life, and God never promises that Christians won't suffer. In fact, serving God can involve putting ourselves in harm's way for the sake of something very important. We actually do our best service when we are stretched beyond our own power and forced to rely on God's power for the strength to continue.

This mystery
In the Bible a mystery isn't a puzzle to solve or a secret to be kept. Rather it's something astonishing that has been kept secret but now can be announced from the rooftops. *Christ* is the great mystery, the surprise that shocked even angels when he became human and died for us.

Has been kept in the dark for a long time
Since the beginning of time, God has been revealing the truth about his ways. God gave Moses and the Israelites much of what we call the Old Testament. God told Moses the history of creation, the Ten Commandments, and detailed instructions about how to worship. As God revealed himself, he made several promises of faithfulness and deliverance. God sent prophets to Israel to remind them of God's ways and to foretell of the coming Messiah. Paul calls the gospel a mystery because until Jesus came, no one fully understood what God was going to do to make good on his promises. Now that Jesus has come, we have the full revelation of God. The mystery is no longer in the dark!

FOR FURTHER STUDY

Matthew 25:14-30

NOTES

If you are watching the LifeTogether DVD, you may use this page to take notes.

APPENDIXES

SPIRITUAL GIFTS

On a scale of 1 to 10, rate your response to each statement. You can then estimate your overall rating for each spiritual gift, or if you prefer to be precise, you can total your ratings for the questions in each section and divide by the number of statements.

GIFTS THAT COMMUNICATE GOD'S WORD

Prophecy 1 Corinthians 14:3
Communicating God's Word publicly or personally in a way that would challenge, comfort, or convict people and point them toward Jesus Christ.

1	2	3	4	5	6	7	8	9	10
NO WAY		DOUBT IT		COULD BE ME		SOUNDS LIKE ME		DEFINITELY ME	

_____ I have given others important messages that I felt came from God at the perfect time.
_____ I think I have the ability to reveal God's truth about the future.
_____ I desire to speak messages from God that will challenge people to change.
_____ I have had the chance to proclaim God's truth at the required time.
_____ I have given messages that were judgments from God.
_____ I think I have the gift of prophecy.

Evangelism Acts 8:26–40
Having spiritual conversations easily and clearly communicating the good news about Jesus Christ naturally to unbelievers who often respond positively with faith.

1	2	3	4	5	6	7	8	9	10
NO WAY		DOUBT IT		COULD BE ME		SOUNDS LIKE ME		DEFINITELY ME	

_____ I can tell nonbelievers about my relationship with Christ in a comfortable manner.

_____ I always think of new ways in which I can share Christ with my unbelieving friends.

_____ I have the ability to direct conversations toward the message of Christ.

_____ I have led others to a personal relationship with Christ.

_____ I desire to learn more about God so I can share him in a clearer way.

_____ I think I have the gift of evangelism.

Missions 1 Corinthians 9:19-23; Acts 13:2-3
Bringing the message of Jesus to a culture or people-group other than your own.

1	2	3	4	5	6	7	8	9	10
NO WAY		DOUBT IT		COULD BE ME		SOUNDS LIKE ME		DEFINITELY ME	

_____ I think I could learn a new language well enough to minister to those in a different culture.

_____ I feel comfortable when I'm around people of a different culture, race, or language.

_____ I adapt easily to a change of settings.

_____ I have a strong desire to see people in other countries won to the Lord.

_____ I am willing to go wherever God wants to send me.

_____ I would like to be a missionary.

Apostleship Romans 15:20
Starting new churches and helping them develop.

1	2	3	4	5	6	7	8	9	10
NO WAY		DOUBT IT		COULD BE ME		SOUNDS LIKE ME		DEFINITELY ME	

_____ I think I can easily adapt to new people and places to accomplish the work God has called me to do.

_____ I am willing to relocate wherever I feel God is calling me to start and develop a church.

_____ I am a visionary and can share my vision with a group of people to lead them in developing a new church.

_____ I have a strong desire to lead others in the planning, development, and implementation of the vision God has given me for starting a church.

_____ I would like to start and develop new churches.

GIFTS THAT EDUCATE GOD'S PEOPLE

Teaching Ephesians 4:12–13
Teaching the Bible to others in a way that causes them to learn and implement life changes.

1	2	3	4	5	6	7	8	9	10
NO WAY		DOUBT IT		COULD BE ME		SOUNDS LIKE ME		DEFINITELY ME	

_____ I enjoy explaining biblical truths to people.

_____ I think I have what it takes to teach a Bible study or lead a small group discussion.

_____ I am willing to spend extra time studying biblical principles in order to communicate them clearly to others.

_____ Because of my teaching, I have brought others to a better understanding of the Christian faith.

_____ Others tell me I present the gospel in a way that is easy to understand.

_____ I think I have the gift of teaching.

Encouragement Acts 14:22
(sometimes called Exhortation)

Caring for others in a way that builds their courage and motivates them to follow Jesus. Also constantly using words and actions to bring out the best in others and to help them feel valued.

1	2	3	4	5	6	7	8	9	10
NO WAY		DOUBT IT		COULD BE ME		SOUNDS LIKE ME		DEFINITELY ME	

_____ I am known for the way I encourage others.
_____ I think I have the ability to comfort those who are off track and help them
        get back on track.
_____ I have a desire to learn more about counseling so I can help others.
_____ I have helped others in their struggles.
_____ I enjoy seeing people respond to encouragement.
_____ I think I have the gift of encouragement.

Wisdom 1 Corinthians 2:1, 6-16
Understanding God's perspective on life situations and sharing these insights in a simple, understand-able way.

1	2	3	4	5	6	7	8	9	10
NO WAY		DOUBT IT		COULD BE ME		SOUNDS LIKE ME		DEFINITELY ME	

_____ My friends view me as a person who is wise.
_____ I think God has given me the ability to make wise decisions.
_____ God has given me the ability to give clear counsel and advice to others.
_____ I am confident that my decisions are in harmony with God's will.
_____ I usually see clear solutions to complicated problems.
_____ I think God has blessed me with the gift of wisdom.

Discernment 1 Corinthians 2:14
Knowing the right responses and actions in nearly all situations.

1	2	3	4	5	6	7	8	9	10
NO WAY		DOUBT IT		COULD BE ME		SOUNDS LIKE ME		DEFINITELY ME	

_____ I have expressed words of truth that have given insights to others.
_____ I desire to fully understand biblical truths.
_____ I am able to help others understand God's Word.
_____ I tend to use biblical insights when I share with others.
_____ I have the ability to learn new insights on my own.
_____ I think I have the gift of discernment.

GIFTS THAT DEMONSTRATE GOD'S LOVE

Service Acts 6:1-7
Giving practical help to others in a way that makes people feel cared for and loved, often behind the scenes and without being asked.

1   2   3   4   5   6   7   8   9   10

NO WAY   DOUBT IT   COULD BE ME   SOUNDS LIKE ME   DEFINITELY ME

_____ I could be described as an other-centered person.
_____ I enjoy meeting the needs of others.
_____ You'll frequently find me volunteering my time to help with the needs
       of the church.
_____ I'm the type of person who likes to reach out to the less fortunate.
_____ I feel good when I help with the routine jobs at church.
_____ I think I have the gift of service.

Mercy Romans 12:8
Showing actions of compassion toward suffering and hurting people; sensing people's feelings and caring for them.

1   2   3   4   5   6   7   8   9   10

NO WAY   DOUBT IT   COULD BE ME   SOUNDS LIKE ME   DEFINITELY ME

_____ I enjoy giving hope to those in need (such as the lonely, elderly, or shut-ins).
_____ I would like to have a ministry with those who are needy.
_____ I would like to visit rest homes and other institutions where people
       need visitors.
_____ I am very compassionate to those in need.
_____ I have a desire to work with people who have special physical needs.
_____ I think I have the gift of mercy.

Hospitality 1 Peter 4:9-10
Making strangers feel welcomed and comfortable; hosting people in your home and making sure they are cared for.

1	2	3	4	5	6	7	8	9	10

NO WAY DOUBT IT COULD BE ME SOUNDS LIKE ME DEFINITELY ME

_____ When people are in need I enjoy having them in my home. I do not feel like they are intruding.

_____ I enjoy having strangers in my home. I like making them feel comfortable.

_____ I think God has given me the ability to make others feel comfortable in my home.

_____ I enjoy providing food and housing to those in need.

_____ I want my house to always be a spot where people in need can come and find rest.

_____ I think I have the gift of hospitality.

Pastoring 1 Peter 5:2-4
(sometimes called shepherding)
Walking with others through life in a caring way that helps them grow in faith; caring for their spiritual needs and helping them develop in their faith.

1	2	3	4	5	6	7	8	9	10

NO WAY DOUBT IT COULD BE ME SOUNDS LIKE ME DEFINITELY ME

_____ I have a way of relating to and comforting those who have fallen away from the Lord.

_____ I try to know people in a personal way so that we feel comfortable with one another.

_____ I would like the responsibilities that my pastor has.

_____ When I teach the Bible, my concern is to see spiritual growth in others.

_____ I would like to be a pastor.

Giving 2 Corinthians 8:1-7
Graciously giving of resources without feeling put out.

1	2	3	4	5	6	7	8	9	10

NO WAY   DOUBT IT   COULD BE ME   SOUNDS LIKE ME   DEFINITELY ME

_____ I see myself as a person who is very generous when it comes to giving money to my church.

_____ I enjoy giving money to the needy.

_____ I have a strong desire to use my money wisely, knowing God will direct my giving.

_____ I cheerfully give my money to others.

_____ I am confident that God will take care of my needs when I give sacrificially and cheerfully.

_____ I think I have the gift of giving.

Miracles Mark 11:23-24
Praying for God's supernatural intervention in impossible situations and seeing God respond.

1	2	3	4	5	6	7	8	9	10

NO WAY   DOUBT IT   COULD BE ME   SOUNDS LIKE ME   DEFINITELY ME

_____ God has used me in a supernatural way to help bring about his will in an impossible situation.

_____ Many incredible acts of God have happened to others through me.

_____ God uses me to perform miracles in his name.

_____ God is glorified when I do miraculous things in his name.

_____ I think I have the gift of miracles.

GIFTS THAT CELEBRATE GOD'S PRESENCE (Worship- and Prayer-Related Gifts)

Healing James 5:14–16
Bringing physical or emotional healing into another's life through prayer.

1	2	3	4	5	6	7	8	9	10

NO WAY   DOUBT IT   COULD BE ME   SOUNDS LIKE ME   DEFINITELY ME

_____ God has used me in a supernatural way to heal someone.
_____ I have healed a disabled person.
_____ I have the ability to heal others.
_____ God is glorified when he heals others through me.
_____ I think I have the gift of healing.

Praying with My Spirit 1 Corinthians 14:13–15
(sometimes called Tongues/Interpretation)
Praying in a language understood only by God or one who interprets the words spoken in that language.

1	2	3	4	5	6	7	8	9	10

NO WAY   DOUBT IT   COULD BE ME   SOUNDS LIKE ME   DEFINITELY ME

_____ I believe I have a prayer language that is unknown to me.
_____ I have spoken in tongues.
_____ When I speak in tongues, I feel God's spirit within me
_____ Others have interpreted my unknown prayer language.
_____ An unknown language comes to me when I'm at a loss for words
        during my prayer time.
_____ I think I have the gift of tongues.

GIFTS THAT SUPPORT ALL THE BIBLICAL PURPOSES

Leadership Hebrews 13:7–17
Setting direction, offering motivation, and giving examples of service to help move a group toward a goal.

1	2	3	4	5	6	7	8	9	10
NO WAY		DOUBT IT		COULD BE ME		SOUNDS LIKE ME		DEFINITELY ME	

_____ I think I know where I am going—and other people seem to follow.

_____ I would enjoy leading, inspiring, and motivating others to become involved in God's work.

_____ I want to lead people to the best solution when they have trouble.

_____ I have influenced others to complete a task or find a biblical answer that helped their lives.

_____ When I'm in a group I'm usually the leader or I take the lead if no one else does.

_____ I think like I have leadership skills.

Administration 1 Corinthians 14:40
(sometimes called organization)
Managing people well and organizing programs and ministries effectively.

1	2	3	4	5	6	7	8	9	10
NO WAY		DOUBT IT		COULD BE ME		SOUNDS LIKE ME		DEFINITELY ME	

_____ I see clearly that a job can be done more effectively if I allow others to assist.

_____ I would enjoy directing a vacation Bible school program or other special event for my church.

_____ I can give others responsibilities for a task or project and help them accomplish it.

_____ I am able to set goals and plan the most effective way to reach them.

_____ I think I have the gift of administration.

Faith Romans 4:18-21

Having a unique amount of trust in God and confidence to act on God's promises; being willing to risk failure in pursuit of a God-given vision, expecting God to handle the obstacles.

1   2   3   4   5   6   7   8   9   10

NO WAY   DOUBT IT   COULD BE ME   SOUNDS LIKE ME   DEFINITELY ME

_____ I often think I know God's will even when others aren't sure.
_____ I enjoy helping others with spiritual needs.
_____ I find it easy to trust God in difficult situations.
_____ I trust God for supernatural miracles.
_____ Others in my group see me as a faithful Christian.
_____ I think I have the gift of faith.

FINDING YOUR S.H.A.P.E.

Spiritual **G**ifts

Heart

Abilities

Personality

Experiences

God has designed you with a unique S.H.A.P.E. that enables you to serve him in ways no other person can. That makes you irreplaceable. When you discover your S.H.A.P.E., you'll have helpful direction toward more specific ways to serve God.

Use this worksheet to help you discover your S.H.A.P.E. By the end of session 6, you'll have all five areas filled out. You'll also have feedback from your group members affirming what they see in you. Use the results as guidelines for choosing a ministry within your church.

FINDING YOUR S.H.A.P.E.: SPIRITUAL GIFTS

Transfer your scores from **Spiritual Gifts** (page 81-90).

_____	Prophecy	_____	Evangelism
_____	Missions	_____	Apostleship
_____	Teaching	_____	Encouragement
_____	Wisdom	_____	Discernment
_____	Service	_____	Mercy
_____	Hospitality	_____	Pastoring
_____	Giving	_____	Miracles
_____	Healing	_____	Praying with My Spirit
_____	Leadership	_____	Administration
_____	Faith		

FINDING YOUR S.H.A.P.E.: HEART AND ABILITIES

Place check marks next to the abilities you believe you have. Be sure to add any natural abilities you think you have that aren't listed.

Circle the things you love to do. Rank your circled choices (1 is your favorite).

◇ Design things
◇ Develop others' ideas
◇ Start new projects
◇ Organize
◇ Serve behind the scenes
◇ Help others
◇ Excel
◇ Entertain
◇ Lead others
◇ Acquire possessions
◇ Compete
◇ Find people for the right tasks
◇ Perform
◇ Research

◇ Improve on ideas
◇ Operate things
◇ Repair stuff
◇ Be in charge
◇ Persevere
◇ Follow the rules
◇ Influence others
◇ Be artistic
◇ Use graphics
◇ Evaluate
◇ Plan
◇ Manage others
◇ Counsel my peers
◇ Teach
◇ Write

◇ Edit
◇ Promote
◇ Repair
◇ Cook
◇ Welcome others
◇ Compose music
◇ Build stuff
◇ Create arts and crafts
◇ Decorate
◇ Play musical instruments
◇ Sing
◇ Others

FINDING YOUR S.H.A.P.E.:

PERSONALITY

Many extensive personality tests are available, but you can get an initial impression about your personality by answering the following questions. Remember, there aren't right and wrong answers. Only honest responses give you an accurate assessment of who you are.

1. Do I tend to be reserved or outgoing?

Few people are exclusively one or the other. Depending on the circumstances, you may switch between the two extremes, but you're likely to have a *preferred* style that's most comfortable for you.

Outgoing people typically…

- are energized by interactions with others.
- love gatherings and are often the last to leave.
- connect with strangers easily.
- pursue relationships with many people at the same time.
- enjoy working with a team of people.

Reserved people typically…

- are drained by long amounts of time with people.
- aren't bothered by being alone.
- like solitary activities.
- are energized by being alone.
- have a limited number of relationships.

Based on these descriptions, I'm probably… (circle one)

OUTGOING   RESERVED

2. Do I tend to make decisions based on facts or feelings?

People who make decisions based on facts typically…

- like facts and trust factual evidence.
- would rather talk about what's real than dream about what could be.
- notice details.
- want people who are telling stories to get to the point.
- like things that are practical, doable, achievable.
- like to reflect and search for the right answers before speaking.

People who make decisions based on feelings typically…

- miss details because their "head is in the clouds."
- think and talk about the future.
- don't care much about the past but love to know what's in the future.
- have good imaginations.
- Like to speculate (ask, *What if…?*) and often have hunches.
- don't care if a choice is practical or not.

Based on these descriptions, I probably make decisions based on (circle one)

FACTS   FEELINGS

3. In my relationships do I tend to be dependent on others or independent?

People who tend to be dependent on others typically...

- 📱 like people around to be happy.
- 📱 have high expectations of others.
- 📱 rely on people to be there for them during tough times.
- 📱 need others to tell them they did good work.
- 📱 need to talk out their feelings.

People who tend to be independent typically...

- 📱 don't need others to be happy.
- 📱 have low expectations of others.
- 📱 rely on themselves to get through tough times.
- 📱 don't rely on others to know they did good work.
- 📱 Figure out their feelings on their own.

Based on these descriptions, I'm probably (circle one)

DEPENDENT   INDEPENDENT

4. Do I prefer to be spontaneous or to plan the use of my time?

People who tend to be spontaneous typically...

- 📱 are flexible about schedule changes.
- 📱 like open-ended situations.
- 📱 don't care about deadlines.
- 📱 are seldom in a rush.

People who tend to prefer planned activities typically...

- 📱 find it difficult to adapt to schedule changes.
- 📱 are organized.
- 📱 plan ahead.
- 📱 like closure.
- 📱 like deadlines.

Based on these descriptions, I'm probably (circle one)

SPONTANEOUS   A PLANNER

FINDING YOUR S.H.A.P.E.:

EXPERIENCES

Transfer your experiences from the timeline on page 60 to the categories below. If you remember additional experiences, write them down too. Then write down the insights you've gained or the lessons you learned from each experience. You may need to come back to this later, because sometimes it takes a while before the lesson comes into focus.

Painful experiences

Family experiences

Spiritual experiences

Ministry experience

SMALL GROUP COVENANT

Read through the following covenant as a group. Discuss concerns and questions. You may modify the covenant based on the needs and concerns of your group members. Those who agree with the terms and are willing to commit themselves to the covenant as you've revised it should sign their own books and the books of everyone entering into the covenant.

A covenant is a binding agreement or contract. God made covenants with Noah, Abraham, and David, among others. Jesus is the fulfillment of a new covenant between God and his people.

If you take your commitment to the Small Group Covenant seriously, you'll find that your group will go deep relationally. Without a covenant you may find yourselves meeting simply for the sake of meeting.

If your group decides to add some additional values (character traits such as be encouraging or be kind), write the new values at the bottom of the covenant page. Your group may also want to create some small group rules (actions such as not interrupting when someone else is speaking or sitting up instead of lying down). You can list those at the bottom of the covenant page also.

Reviewing your group's covenant, values, and rules before each meeting will become a significant part of your small group experience.

OUR COVENANT

I, _____ , as a member of our small group, acknowledge my need for meaningful relationships with other believers. I agree that this small group community exists to help me deepen my relationships with God, Christians, and other people in my life. I commit to the following:

Consistency I will give my best effort to attend every time our small group meets.

Honesty I will take risks to share truthfully about the personal issues in my life.

Confidentiality I will support the foundation of trust in our small group by not participating in gossip. I will not reveal personal information shared by others during our meetings.

Respect I will help create a safe environment for our small group members by listening carefully and not making fun of others.

Prayer I will make a committed effort to pray regularly for the people in our small group.

Accountability I will allow the people in my small group to hold me accountable for growing spiritually and living a life that honors God.

This covenant, signed by all the members in this group, reflects our commitment to one another.

Signature	Date
Signature	Date
Signature	Date
Signature	Date
Signature	Date
Signature	Date
Signature	Date
Signature	Date
Signature	Date

SMALL GROUP Roster

name	EMAIL

Phone	AdDresS	schOol & GRADE

HOW TO KEEP YOUR SMALL GROUP FROM BECOMING A CLIQUE

Cliques arise naturally because we all want to belong—God created us to be connected in community with one another. The same drive that creates community creates cliques. A clique isn't just a group of friends, but a group of friends uninterested in anyone outside the group. Cliques result in pain for those who are excluded.

If you reread the first paragraph of the introduction **"Read Me First"** (page 9), you see the words *spiritual community* used to describe your small group. If your small group becomes a clique, it's an *unspiritual* community. You have a clique when the biblical purpose of fellowship turns inward. That's ugly. It's the opposite of what God intended the body of Christ to be.

- Cliques make your youth ministry look bad.
- Cliques make your small group appear immature.
- Cliques hurt the feelings of excluded people.
- Cliques contradict the value God places on each person.
- Few things are as unappealing as a youth ministry filled with cliques.

Many leaders avoid using small groups as a means toward spiritual growth because they fear the groups will become cliquish. But when they're healthy, small groups can improve the well-being, friendliness, and depth of your youth ministry.

> **Be wise in the way you act toward outsiders; make the most of every opportunity.**
>
> —Colossians 4:5

Here are some ideas for preventing your small group from turning into a clique:

Be Aware

Learn to recognize when people feel like they don't fit in with your group. It's easy to forget when you're an insider how bad it feels to be an outsider.

Reach Out

Once you're aware of a person feeling left out, make efforts to be friendly. Smile, shake hands, say hello, ask them to sit with you or your group, and ask simple yet personalized questions. A person who feels like an outsider may come across as defensive, so be as accepting as possible.

Launch New Small Groups

Any small group that has the attitude of "us four and no more" has become a clique. A time will come when your small group should launch into multiple small groups if it gets too big. The bigger a small group gets, the less healthy it will become. If your small group understands this, there will be a culture of growth instead of cliques. New or introverted people often are affected by cliques because they have a hard time breaking through the existing connections that the small group members already have. When you start new groups you'll see fellowship move from ugly to what God intended—a practical extension of his love.

Challenge Others

Small group members expect adult leaders to confront them for acting like a clique. Instead of waiting for an adult to make the move, shock everyone by stepping up and challenging what you know is destructive. Take a risk. Be a spokesperson for your youth ministry and your student peers by leading the way—be part of a small group that isn't cliquey and one who isn't afraid to challenge the groups who are.

By practicing these key ideas, your group will excel at reaching out to others and deepening the biblical fellowship within your church.

ACCOUNTABILITY QUESTIONS

During your small group time, you'll have opportunities to connect with one other person in the group—your spiritual partner. Relationships can go deeper if you have the same partner for the entire book or even the entire LIFETOGETHER series. Be as mellow as you want or crank it up to a higher level by talking throughout the week and checking in with each other about your spiritual journeys.

For those who want to go to a deeper level with their spiritual partners, here's a list of questions you can use as a guide for accountability. Depending on the time you have available, you might discuss all of them or only a couple.

The Wonder Question
Have you maintained an attitude of awe and wonder toward God?
(Have you minimized him? Placed him in a box? Forgotten to consider his character?)

The Priority Question
Have you maintained a personal devotional time (quiet time) with God?
(Have you allowed yourself to become too busy? Filled your life with too much activity?)

The Morality Question
Have you maintained integrity in the way you live?
(Have you compromised your integrity or the truth with your actions? Your thoughts? Your words?)

The Listening Question
Are you sensitive to the promptings and leading of the Holy Spirit?
(Have you drowned out his voice with too much noise?)

The Relationships Question

Have you maintained peaceful relationships and resolved conflicts to the best of your ability? (Have you caused conflict, offended others, or avoided resolving tension?)

The Prayer Question

How can I pray for you this week?

E valuating your spiritual journey is a good thing. Parts of your journey will take you to low spots, while others will lead you to high places. Spiritual growth is not a smooth incline—loopy roller coaster is more like it. When you regularly consider your life, you'll develop an awareness of God's Spirit working in you. Evaluate. Think. Learn. Grow.

The assessment in this section is a tool, not a test. The purpose of this tool is to help you evaluate where you're at in your faith journey. No one is perfect in this life, so don't worry about what score you get. It won't be published in your church bulletin. Be honest so you have an accurate idea of how you're doing.

When you finish, celebrate the areas where you're relatively healthy, and think about how you can use your strengths to help others on their spiritual journeys. Then think of ways your small group members can aid one another to improve weak areas through support and example.

 FELLOWSHIP: CONNECTING Your Heart to Others'

1. I meet consistently with a small group of Christians.

1	2	3	4	5
poor				outstanding

2. I'm connected to other Christians who hold me accountable.

1	2	3	4	5
poor				outstanding

3. I can talk with my small group leader when I need help, advice, or support.

1	2	3	4	5
poor				outstanding

4. My Christian friends are a significant source of strength and stability in my life.

1	2	3	4	5
poor				outstanding

5. I regularly pray for others in my small group between meetings.

1	2	3	4	5
poor				outstanding

6. I have resolved all conflicts I have had with other Christians and non–Christians.

1	2	3	4	5
poor				outstanding

7. I've done all I possibly can to be a good son or daughter and brother or sister.

1	2	3	4	5
poor				outstanding

Take time to answer the following questions to further evaluate your spiritual health (after your small group meets if you don't have time during the meeting). If you need help with this, schedule a time with your small group leader to talk about your spiritual health.

8. List the three most significant relationships you have right now. Why are these people important to you?

9. How would you describe the benefit you receive from being in fellowship with other Christians?

SERVING others in love

Do you have an accountability partner? If so, what have you been doing to hold each other accountable? If not, how can you get one?

DISCIPLESHIP: GROWING to Be Like Jesus

11. I have regular times of conversation with God.

1	2	3	4	5
poor				outstanding

12. I'm a closer friend with God this month than I was last month.

1	2	3	4	5
poor				outstanding

13. I'm making better decisions this month when compared to last month.

1	2	3	4	5
poor				outstanding

14. I regularly attend church services and grow spiritually as a result.

1	2	3	4	5
poor				outstanding

15. I consistently honor God with my finances through giving.

1	2	3	4	5
poor				outstanding

16. I regularly study the Bible on my own.

1	2	3	4	5
poor				outstanding

17. I regularly memorize Bible verses or passages.

1	2	3	4	5
poor				outstanding

Take time to answer the following questions to further evaluate your spiritual health (after your small group meets if you don't have time during the meeting). If you need help with this, schedule a time with your small group leader to talk about your spiritual health.

What books or chapters from the Bible have you read during the last month?

What has God been teaching you from Scripture lately?

What was the last verse you memorized? When did you memorize it? Describe the last time a memorized Bible verse helped you.

MINISTRY: SERVING Others in Love

21. I am currently serving in some ministry capacity.

1	2	3	4	5
poor				outstanding

22. I'm effectively ministering where I'm serving.

1	2	3	4	5
poor				outstanding

23. Generally I have a humble attitude when I serve others.

1	2	3	4	5
poor				outstanding

24. I understand God has created me as a unique individual and he has a special plan for my life.

1	2	3	4	5
poor				outstanding

25. When I help others, I typically don't look for anything in return.

1	2	3	4	5
poor				outstanding

26. My family and friends consider me to be generally unselfish.

1	2	3	4	5
poor				outstanding

27. I'm usually sensitive to the hurts of others and respond in a caring way.

1	2	3	4	5
poor				outstanding

Take time to answer the following questions to further evaluate your spiritual health (after your small group meets if you don't have time during the meeting). If you need help with this, schedule a time with your small group leader to talk about your spiritual health.

If you're currently serving in a ministry, why are you serving? If not, what's kept you from getting involved?

What spiritual lessons have you learned while serving?

What frustrations have you experienced as a result of serving?

EVANGELISM: SHARING Your Story and God's Story

31. I regularly pray for my non-Christian friends.

1	2	3	4	5
poor				outstanding

32. I invite my non-Christian friends to church.

1	2	3	4	5
poor				outstanding

33. I talk about my faith with others.

1	2	3	4	5
poor				outstanding

34. I pray for opportunities to share about what Jesus has done in my life.

1	2	3	4	5
poor				outstanding

35. People know I'm a Christian by more than my words.

1	2	3	4	5
poor				outstanding

36. I feel a strong compassion for non-Christians.

1	2	3	4	5
poor				outstanding

37. I have written out my testimony and am ready to share it.

1	2	3	4	5
poor				outstanding

Take time to answer the following questions to further evaluate your spiritual health (after your small group meets if you don't have time during the meeting). If you need help with this, schedule a time with your small group leader to talk about your spiritual health.

Describe any significant spiritual conversations you've had with unbelievers in the past month.

Has your faith been challenged by any non-Christians? If yes, how?

What have been some difficulties you've faced with sharing your faith?

What successes have you experienced recently in personal evangelism? (Success isn't limited to bringing people to salvation directly. Helping someone take a step closer at any point on his or her spiritual journey is success.)

WORSHIP: SURRENDERING Your Life to Honor God

42. I consistently participate in Sunday and midweek worship experiences at church.

1	2	3	4	5
poor				outstanding

43. My heart breaks over the things that break God's heart.

1	2	3	4	5
poor				outstanding

44. I regularly give thanks to God.

1	2	3	4	5
poor				outstanding

45. I'm living a life that, overall, honors God.

1	2	3	4	5
poor				outstanding

46. I have an attitude of wonder and awe toward God.

1	2	3	4	5
poor				outstanding

48. I use the free access I have into God's presence often.

1	2	3	4	5
poor				outstanding

Take time to answer the following questions to further evaluate your spiritual health (after your small group meets if you don't have time during the meeting). If you need help with this, schedule a time with your small group leader to talk about your spiritual health.

Make a list of your top five priorities. You can get a good idea of your priorities by evaluating how you spend your time. Be realistic and honest. Are your priorities in the right order? Do you need to get rid of some or add new priorities? (As a student you may have some limitations. This isn't ammo for dropping out of school or disobeying parents!)

List ten things you're thankful for. **50**

51 What influences, directs, guides, or controls you the most?

DAILY BIBLE READINGS

As you meet together with your small group friends for Bible study, prayer, and encouragement, you'll grow spiritually. No matter how deep your friendships go, you're not likely to be together for your entire lives, so you need to learn to grow spiritually on your own too. God has given you an incredible tool to help—his love letter, the Bible. The Bible reveals God's love for you and gives directions for living life to the fullest.

To help you, you'll find a collection of Bible passages that reinforce each week's lesson below. Every day *read* the daily verses, *reflect* on how the verses inspire or challenge you, and *respond* to God through prayer or by writing in your journal or on the journaling pages in this book.

Check off the passages as you read them. Don't feel guilty if you miss a daily reading. Simply do your best to develop the habit of being in God's Word daily.

☐ Week 1
1 Corinthians 15:58
Ephesians 2:4-10
Isaiah 45:9-12
Genesis 1:27-31
Psalm 8:3-9

☐ Week 2
Matthew 20:20-28
Luke 14:7-11
Luke 14:12-14
John 13:1-11
John 13:12-17

☐ Week 3
1 Peter 4:10-11
Ephesians 4:11-13
1 Corinthians 12:4-11
Romans 12:4-8
Acts 20:24

☐ Week 4
Matthew 5:13-16
Job 10:8-12
Jeremiah 1:4-8
Amos 7:12-15
Judges 6:11-16

☐ Week 5
1 Corinthians 10:31
Acts 20:24
2 Timothy 1:6-7
Philippians 3:12-14
Romans 8:28

☐ Week 6
Colossians 3:22-24
Ephesians 6:5-8
Esther 4:12-16
1 Kings 8:61
Deuteronomy 30:11-20

HOW TO STUDY THE BIBLE

The Bible is the foundation of all the books in the LIFETOGETHER series. Every lesson contains a passage from the Bible for your small group to study and apply. To maximize the impact of your small group experience, it's helpful if each participant spends time reading and studying the Bible during the week. When you read the Bible for yourself, you can have discussions based on what *you* know the Bible says instead of what another member has heard second- or third-hand about the Bible. You also minimize the risk of depending on your small group for all your Bible study time.

Growing Christians learn to study the Bible on their own so they can learn to grow on their own. Here are some principles about studying the Bible to help you give God's Word a central place in your life.

Choose a Time and Place

Since we're so easily distracted, pick a time when you're at your best. If you're a morning person, then give that time to study the Bible. Find a place away from phones, computers, and TVs, so you are less likely to be interrupted.

Begin with Prayer

Make an effort to acknowledge God's presence. Thank him for his gifts, confess your sins, and ask for his guidance and understanding as you study his love letter to you.

Start with Excitement

We easily take God's Word for granted and forget what an incredible gift we have. God wasn't forced to reach out to us, but he did. He's made it possible for us to know him, understand his directions, and be encouraged, all through the Bible. Remind yourself how amazing it is that God wants you to know him.

Read the Passage

After choosing a passage, read it several times. You might want to read it slowly, pausing after each sentence. If possible, read it out loud. Originally the Bible was heard, not read.

Keep a Journal

Respond to God's Word by writing down how you're challenged, truths you want to remember, thanksgiving and praise, sins to confess, commands to obey, or any other thoughts you have.

Dig Deep

When you read the Bible, look deeper than the plain meaning of the words. Here are a few ideas about what you might find.

Truth about God's character
What do the verses reveal about God's character?

Truth about your life and our world
You don't have to figure out life on your own. Life can be difficult, but when you know how the world works you can make good decisions guided by wisdom from God.

Truth about the world's past
The Bible reveals God's intervention in our mistakes and triumphs throughout history. The choices we read about—good and bad—serve as examples to challenge us to greater faith and obedience. (See Hebrews 11:1-12:1.)

Truth about our actions
God will never leave you stranded. Although he allows us to go through hard times, he is always with us. Our actions have consequences and rewards. Just like he does in Bible stories, God can use all of the consequences and rewards caused by our actions to help others.

As you read, ask these four questions to help you learn from the Bible:

- What do these verses teach me about who God is, how he acts, and how people respond?
- What does this passage teach about the nature of the world?

- What wisdom can I learn from what I read?
- How should I change my life because of what I learned from these verses?

Ask Questions

You may be tempted to skip over parts you don't understand, but don't give up too easily. Understanding the Bible can be hard work. If you come across a word you don't know, look it up in a regular dictionary or a Bible dictionary. If you come across a verse that seems to contradict another verse, see whether your Bible has any notes to explain it. Write down your questions and ask someone who has more knowledge about the Bible than you. Buy or borrow a study Bible or check the Internet. Try these sites to begin with:

www.twopaths.com
www.gotquestions.org
www.carm.org

Apply the Truth to Your Life

The Bible should make a difference in your life. It contains the help you need to live the life God intended. Knowledge of the Bible without personal obedience is worthless and causes hypocrisy and pride. Take time to consider the condition of your thinking, attitudes, and actions, and wonder about how God is working in you. Think about your life situation and how you can serve others better.

More Helpful Ideas

- Take the position that the times you have set aside for Bible reading and study are nonnegotiable. Don't let other activities squeeze Bible study time out of your schedule.
- Avoid the extremes of being ritualistic (reading a chapter just to mark it off a list) and lazy (giving up).
- Begin with realistic goals and boundaries for your study time. Five to seven minutes a day may be a challenge for you at the beginning.
- Be open to the leading and teaching of God's Spirit.
- Love God like he's your parent (or the parent you wish you had).

MEMORY VERSES

The word *memory* may cause some people to throw this book and kick the dog. Throughout your school years, you have to memorize dates, places, times, and outcomes. Now we're telling you to memorize the Bible?! Seriously?

Not the entire Bible. Start with some key verses. Here's why: Scripture memorization is a good habit for a growing Christian to develop. When God's Word is planted in your mind and heart, it has a way of influencing how you live. King David understood this when he wrote; " I have hidden your word in my heart that I might not sin against you" (Psalm 119:11).

Challenge one another in your small group to memorize the six verses below— one for each time your small group meets. Hold each other accountable by asking about one another's progress. Write the verses on index cards and keep them handy so you can learn and review them when you have free moments (standing in line, before class starts, when you've finished a test and others are still working, waiting for your dad to get out of the bathroom…). You'll be surprised at how many verses you can memorize as you work toward this goal and add verses to your list.

Week 1

I praise you because I am fearfully
and wonderfully made;
your works are wonderful,
I know that full well.

—Psalm 139:14

Week 2

"Whoever wants to become
great among you
must be your servant."

—Mark 10:43

Each one of you should use whatever gift
he has received to serve others,
faithfully administering God's grace
in its various forms.

—1 Peter 4:10

For this reason I remind you
to fan into flame the gift of God,
which is in you through the laying
on of my hands.

—2 Timothy 1:6

"You intended to harm me,
but God intended it for good to accomplish
what is now being done,
the saving of many lives."

—Genesis 50:20

Jesus looked at them and said,
"With man this is impossible,
but with God
all things are possible."

—Matthew 19:26

JOURNALING: SNAPSHOTS OF YOUR HEART

n the simplest terms, journaling is reflection with pen in hand. A growing life needs time to reflect, so several times throughout the book you're asked to reflect in writing, and you always have a journaling option at the end of each session. Through these writing opportunities, you're getting a taste of what it means to journal.

When you take time to write reflections in a journal, you'll experience many benefits. A journal is more than a diary. It's a series of snapshots of your heart. The goal of journaling is to slow down your life to capture some of the great, crazy, wonderful, chaotic, painful, encouraging, angering, confusing, joyful, and loving thoughts, feelings and ideas that enter your life. Writing in a journal can become a powerful habit when you reflect on your life and how God is working.

You'll find room to journal on the following pages.

Personal Insights

When confusion abounds in your life, disorderly thoughts and feelings can become like wild animals. They often loom just out of range, slightly out of focus, but never gone from your awareness. Putting these thoughts and feelings on paper is like corralling and domesticating the wild beasts. Then you can look at them, consider them, contemplate the reasons they were causing you pain, and learn from them.

Have you ever had trouble answering the question, "How do you feel?" Journaling compels you to become more specific with your generalized thoughts and feelings. This is not to suggest that a page full of words perfectly represents what's happening on the inside. That would be foolish. But journaling can move you closer to understanding more about yourself.

Reflection and Examination

With journaling, once you recognize what you're to write about, you can then consider its value. You can write about your feelings, your situations, how you responded to events. You can reflect and answer questions like these:

- Was that the right response?
- What were my other options?
- Did I lose control and act impulsively?
- If this happened again, should I do the same thing? Would I do the same thing?
- How can I be different as a result of this situation?

Spiritual Insights

One of the main goals of journaling is to learn new spiritual insights about God, yourself, and the world. When you take time to journal, you have the opportunity to pause and consider how God is working in your life and in the lives of those around you, so you don't miss the work he's accomplishing. And journaling helps you remember.

What to Write

There isn't one way to journal, no set number of times per week, no rules for the length of each journal entry. Figure out what works best for you. Get started with these options:

A letter or prayer to God

Many Christians struggle with maintaining a consistent prayer life. Writing out your prayers can help strengthen it. Begin with this question: *What do I want to tell God right now?*

A letter to or a conversation with another person

Sometimes conversations with others can be difficult because we're not sure what we ought to say. Have you ever walked away from an interaction and 20 minutes later think, *I should have said…?* Journaling conversations before they happen can help you think through the issues and be intentional in your interactions with others. As a result, you can feel confident as you begin your conversations because you've taken time to consider the issues.

Conflict and pain

You may find it helpful to write about your conflicts with others, especially those that take you by surprise. By journaling soon after, you can reflect and learn from the conflicts. You'll be better prepared for the next time you face a similar situation. Conflicts are generally difficult to navigate. Thinking through the interactions typically yields helpful personal insights.

When you're experiencing pain is a good time to settle your

thoughts and consider the nature of your feelings. The great thing about exploring your feelings is that you're only accountable to God. You don't have to worry about hurting anyone's feelings by what you write in your journal (if you keep it private).

Personal motivation

The Bible is clear regarding two heart truths:

- How you act is a reflection of who you are on the inside (Luke 6:45).
- You can take the right action for the wrong reason (James 4:3).

The condition of your heart is so important. Molding your motives to God's desire is central to being a follower of Christ. The Pharisees did many of the right things, but for the wrong reasons. Reflect on the *real* reasons you do what you do.

Personal Impact

Have you ever gone to bed thinking, *That was a mistake. I didn't intend for that to happen!?* Probably! No one is perfect. You can't predict all of the consequences of your actions. Reflecting on how your actions impact others will help you relate better to others.

God's work in your life

If you write in your journal in the evening, you can answer this question: *What did God teach me today?*

If you journal in the morning, you can answer this question: *God, what were you trying to teach me yesterday that I missed?* When you reflect on yesterday's events, you may find a common theme that God may have been weaving into your life during the day, one you missed because you were busy. When you see God's hand in your life, even a day later, you know God loves you and is guiding you.

Scripture

Journal about whatever you learn from the Bible. Rewrite a verse in your own words, or figure out how a passage is structured. Try to uncover the key truths from the verses and figure out how the verses apply to your life.

SCRIBBLES

SCRIBBLES

This is the one who warned the so!
Who heeded the snar!
And sought from the rat!
When did the drug
That led the rabbit that lived huh.
That a lion looked the rabbit that lived huh.
When did the one

Genesi

SCRIBBLES

SCRIBBLES

JOURNALING page

PRAYING IN YOUR SMALL GROUP

As believers, we're called to support one another in prayer, and prayer should become a consistent part of creating a healthy small group.

One of the purposes of prayer is to align our hearts with God's. By doing this, we can more easily think his thoughts and feel his feelings—in our limited human way. Prayer shouldn't be a how-well-did-I-do performance or a self-conscious, put-on-the-spot task to fear. Your small group may need time to get comfortable with praying out loud. That's okay.

Follow Jesus' Example

When you do pray, silently or aloud, follow the practical, simple words of Jesus in Matthew 6.

Pray sincerely.

"And when you pray, do not be like the hypocrites, for they love to pray standing in the synagogues and on the street corners to be seen by men. I tell you the truth, they have received their reward in full."

—Matthew 6:5

In the Old Testament, God's people were disciplined prayer warriors. They developed specific prayers to use for every special occasion or need. They had prayers for light and darkness, prayers for fire and rain, prayers for good news and bad. They even had prayers for travel, holidays, holy days, and Sabbath days.

Every day the faithful would stop to pray at 9:00 A.M., noon, and 3:00 P.M., a sort of religious coffee break. Their ritual was impressive, to say the least, but being legalistic has its downside. The proud, self-righteous types would strategically plan their schedules to be in the middle of a crowd when it was time for prayer so everyone could hear them as they prayed loudly. You can see the problem. What was intended to promote spiritual passion became a drama for the crowd.

The Lord wants our prayers addressed to him alone. That seems obvious enough, yet how many of us pray more with the need to impress our listeners than to communicate with God? This is the problem if you're prideful like the Pharisees about the excellent quality of your prayers. But it can also be a problem if you're new to prayer and concerned that you don't know how to "pray right." Don't concern yourself with what others think; just talk to God as if you were sitting in a chair next to him.

Pray simply.

"And when you pray, do not keep on babbling like pagans, for they think they will be heard because of their many words. Do not be like them, for your Father knows what you need before you ask him."

—Matthew 6:7-8

The Lord doesn't ask to be dazzled with brilliantly crafted language. Nor is he impressed with lengthy monologues. It's freeing to know that he wants us to keep it simple.

Pray specifically.

"This, then, is how you should pray: 'Our Father in heaven, hallowed be your name, your kingdom come, your will be done on earth as it is in heaven. Give us today our daily bread. Forgive us our debts, as we also have forgiven our debtors. And lead us not into temptation, but deliver us from the evil one.'"

—Matthew 6:9-13

What the church has come to call **The Lord's Prayer** is a model of the kind of brief but specific prayers we may offer anytime, anywhere. Look at some of the specific items mentioned:

Adoration—hallowed be your name

Provision—your kingdom come...your will be done...give us today our daily bread

Forgiveness—forgive us our debts

Protection—lead us not into temptation

PRAYER REQUEST GUIDLINES

Because prayer time is so vital, small group members need to know some basic guidelines for sharing, handling, and praying for prayer requests. Without a commitment from each person to honor these simple suggestions, prayer time can be dominated by one person, be a gossipfest, or be a never-ending story time. (There are appropriate times to tell personal stories, but this may not be the best time.)

Here are a few suggestions for each group to consider:

Write the requests down.

Each small group member should write down every prayer request on the **Prayer Request Log** (pages 132-137). When you commit to a small group, you're agreeing to be part of the spiritual community, which includes praying for one another. By keeping track of prayer requests, you can be aware of how God answers them. You'll be amazed at God's power and faithfulness.

As an alternative, one person can record the requests and e-mail them to the rest of the group. If your group chooses this option, *safeguard confidentiality.* Be sure personal information isn't compromised. Some people share e-mail accounts with parents or siblings. Develop a workable plan for this option.

Give everyone an opportunity to share.

As a group, be mindful of the amount of time remaining and the number of people who still want to share. You won't be able to share every thought or detail about a situation.

Obviously if someone experiences a crisis, you may need to focus exclusively on that group member by giving him or her extended time and focused prayer. (However, *true* crises are infrequent.)

The leader can limit the time by making a comment such as one of the following:

- Everyone can share one praise or request.
- Simply tell us what to pray for. We can talk more later.
- We're only going to pray for requests about the people in our group.
- We've run out of time to share prayer requests. Take a moment to write down your prayer request and give it to me [or identify another person]. You'll get them by e-mail tomorrow.

Just as people are free to share, they're free to not share.

The goal of a healthy small group should be to create an environment where participants feel comfortable sharing about their lives. Still, not everyone needs to share each week. Here's what I tell my small group:

> As a small group we're here to support one another in prayer. This doesn't mean that everyone has to share something. In fact, I don't want you to think, *I've got to share something.* There's no need to make up prayer requests just to have something to say. If you have something you'd like the group to pray for, let us know. If not, that's fine too.

No gossip allowed.

Don't allow sharing prayer requests to become an excuse for gossip. This is easy to do if you all aren't careful. If you're not part of the problem or solution, consider the information gossip. Sharing the request without the story behind it helps prevent gossip. Also speak in general terms without giving names or details ("I have a friend who's in trouble. God knows who it is. Pray for me that I can be a good friend.").

If a prayer request starts going astray, someone should kindly intercede, perhaps with a question such as, "How can we pray for *you* in this situation?"

Don't give advice or try to fix the problem.

When people share their struggles and problems, a common response is to try to fix the problem by offering advice. At the right time, the group might provide input on a particular problem, but during prayer time, keep focused on praying for the need. Often God's best work in a person's life comes through times of struggle and pain.

Keep in touch.

Make sure you exchange phone numbers and emails before you leave the first meeting, so you can contact someone who needs prayer or encouragement before the next time your group meets. You can write each person's contact information on the **Small Group Roster** (page 98).

During the Small Group Gathering

- One person closes in prayer for the entire group.
- Pray silently. Have one person close the silent prayer time after a while with *Amen.*
- The leader or other group member prays out loud for each person in the group.
- Everyone prays for one request or person. This can be done randomly during prayer or, as the request is shared, a willing pray-er can announce, "I'll pray for that."
- Everyone who wants to pray takes a turn or two. Not everyone needs to pray out loud.
- Split the group into half and pray together in a smaller group.
- Pair up and pray for each other.
- On occasion, each person can share what he or she is thankful for before a prayer request, so prayer requests don't become negative from focusing only on problems. Prayer isn't just asking for stuff. It includes praising God and being thankful for his generosity toward us.

■ If you're having an animated discussion about a Bible passage or a life situation, don't feel like you *must* cut it short for prayer requests. Use it as an opportunity to add a little variety to the prayer time by praying some *other* day between sessions.

Outside the Group Time

You can use these options if you run out of time to pray during the meeting or in addition to prayer during the meeting.

■ Send prayer requests to each other via e-mail.
■ Pick partners and phone each other.
■ Have each person in the small group choose a day to pray for everyone in the group. Perhaps you can work it out to have each day of the week covered. Let participants report back at each meeting for accountability.
■ Have each person pray for just one other person in the group for the entire week. (Everyone prays for the person on the left or on the right or draw names.)

PRAYER REQUEST LOG

DATE	who shared	ReQuest	r8sponse/ anSweR

PRAYER REQUEST LOG

DATE	who shared	ReQuest	r8sponse/ anSweR

PRAYER REQUEST LOG

DATE	who shared	ReQuest	rEsponse/ anSweR

PRAYER REQUEST LOG

DATE	who shared	ReQuest	rEspønse/ anSweR

PRAYER REQUEST LOG

DATE	who shared	REQUEST	rEspOnsE/ anSwER

PRAYER REQUEST LOG

DATE	who shared	ReQuest	r&sponse/anSweR

Your group will benefit the most if you work through the entire LIFETOGETHER series. The longer your group is together, the better your chances of maturing spiritually and integrating the biblical purposes into your life. Here's a plan to complete the series in one year.

I recommend you begin with **STARTING to Go Where God Wants You to Be**, because it contains an introduction to each of the five biblical purposes (though it isn't mandatory). You can use the rest of the books in any order.

As you look at your youth ministry calendar, you may want to use the books in the order they complement events the youth group will be participating in. For example, if you plan to have an evangelism outreach in the fall, study **SHARING Your Story and God's Story** first to build momentum. Study **SERVING Others in Love** in late winter to prepare for the spring break missions' trip.

Use your imagination to celebrate the completion of each book. Have a worship service, an outreach party, a service project, a fun night out, a meet-the-family dinner, or whatever else you can dream up.

SERVING others in love

Number of weeks	Meeting topic
1	Planning meeting—a casual gathering to get acquainted, discuss expectations, and refine the covenant (see page 88).
6	**STARTING to Go Where God Wants You to Be**
1	Celebration
6	**CONNECTING Your Heart to Others'**
1	Celebration
6	**SHARING Your Story and God's Story**
1	Celebration
6	**GROWING to Be Like Jesus**
1	Celebration
6	**SERVING Others in Love**
1	Celebration
6	**SURRENDERING Your Life to Honor God**
1	Celebration
2	Christmas break
1	Easter break
6	Summer break
52	One year

ABOUT THE AUTHORS

Doug Fields, founder of Simply Youth Ministry, has been in youth ministry since 1979 and is currently on staff at Saddleback Church in Southern California. He's the director of Purpose Driven Youth Ministry, and the author and coauthor of more than 50 books, including the bestsellers *Speaking to Teenagers* and *Your First Two Years in Youth Ministry.*

Brett Eastman is pastor of membership and small groups at Saddleback Church, where there are now over 1,500 small group leaders and a growing network of volunteer coaches and bivocational pastors. Brett created the Healthy Small Group strategy and he leads the Large Church Small Group Forums for the Leadership Network. Brett is coauthor of the DOING LIFE TOGETHER Bible study series. Brett and his wife, Dee, have five children.

CPSIA information can be obtained at www.ICGtesting.com
Printed in the USA
LVOW051139150213

320069LV00004B/9/P